Pastor, I Have a Question

Answers to challenging questions about the Bible and the Christian life

Paul LeBoutillier

Copyright © 2023 by Paul LeBoutillier

All rights reserved.

No portion of this book may be reproduced in any form without written permission from the publisher or author, except as permitted by U.S. copyright law.

Unless otherwise indicated, Scripture quotations are from the ESV® Bible (The Holy Bible, English Standard Version®), copyright © 2001 by Crossway, a publishing ministry of Good News Publishers. Used by permission. All rights reserved.

Scripture quotations marked (NIV) are taken from the Holy Bible, New International Version®, NIV®. Copyright © 1973, 1978, 1984, 2011 by Biblica, Inc.™ Used by permission of Zondervan. All rights reserved worldwide. www.zondervan.com

Cover design by Juaquin Pineda
Cover photo by Debi Graniela (@shutterbug_debi)

Printed in the United States of America

To all who have a heart to truly know what God's Word says
and who are not afraid to ask questions
in their pursuit of truth.

For the LORD gives wisdom;
from his mouth come knowledge and understanding.
Proverbs 2:6

Contents

Introduction	VII
Preface	IX
1. SALVATION	1
2. OUR STRUGGLE WITH SIN	28
3. FORGIVING OTHERS	37
4. MAKING DECISIONS	47
5. HOW SHOULD WE RESPOND TO...	59
6. THE CHRISTIAN LIFE	70
7. PRAYER	100
8. MARRIAGE	113
9. SPIRITUAL GIFTS	128
10. WHAT DOES THE BIBLE SAY ABOUT...	136
11. OLD TESTAMENT AND THE LAW OF MOSES	173
12. THE HOLY TRINITY	196
13. GOD	201

14.	JESUS	214
15.	HOLY SPIRIT	230
16.	LAST DAYS	238
17.	ON DEATH AND GOING TO HEAVEN	244
18.	QUESTIONS ABOUT THE BIBLE	256
19.	MISCELLANEOUS QUESTIONS	265

Introduction

In many cases, writers and editors end up being friends.

But how would you describe the dynamic between two good friends who one day decide to publish a book?

There can be many answers to this, but in the context of co-laboring for the advancement of the Kingdom, I could not agree more with this statement made by A.W. Tozer in his introduction to his book, *Born After Midnight*:

> "If there is anything here good or helpful to the children of God, it must be attributed to the operation of the Holy Spirit who often condescends to work through unworthy instruments."

We are unworthy instruments – this is just one of the many things Pastor Paul and I have come to learn and learn all over again while putting this book together; and until now we stand in awe at the "depth of the riches and wisdom and knowledge of God" (Romans 11:33) who has it in his great and wise heart to involve us in what He is doing.

Serving alongside Pastor Paul in making this book has been a delight.

viii   PASTOR, I HAVE A QUESTION

It is my hope that as you read it, the Holy Spirit will stir within you an even greater hunger for the Word. I pray that as you gain insight from these pages, you'll ask the Lord to teach you in the way you should go and give you an undivided heart — a heart set on things above, a heart that day by day grows in its understanding of the infinite and incomparable worth of knowing Christ Jesus our Lord.

Janine Pineda
Editor

Preface

It was in 2011 when one of our audio-visual techs at CCO suggested we start uploading my Bible teachings to YouTube so that our members could catch up on anything they might have missed. Back then it never occurred to us that people who weren't attending our fellowship would *ever* take notice of my studies through the Bible. But as time went on, with more and more people outside our fellowship tuning in, we discovered that there was a spiritual hunger for verse-by-verse Bible teaching that we had completely underestimated.

Because of the online exposure those studies were now getting, I started receiving emails from people all over the world seeking more insight on various Bible-related topics. I've always tried my best to respond to every email I get, but I observed that some questions were either very similar or identical to the ones I had already answered. This gave me the idea to start publishing questions and answers to a blog.

During a video conversation with Janine, the idea came into our hearts to turn those questions and answers into a book. She offered what I have come to appreciate as her considerable editorial talents and the rest you have in your hands.

x   PASTOR, I HAVE A QUESTION

Some of the questions in this book are strictly biblical and seek to better understand the meaning of Scripture, while others lean toward gaining a better philosophical understanding of what God expects from His children. You will find a great many questions for which there is no specific response within the pages of Scripture. For these, I am forced to rely on a "sanctified conscience" (to borrow a phrase from a brother in Christ) or just a general acquaintance with the heart of God.

Although I am a Bible teacher, I do not consider myself a scholar. I simply don't have that level of education. (I'm aware of other much more qualified men and women who are at this time answering Bible questions and I deeply appreciate their labor for the Lord.) What I bring to the discussion is quite simply a man who loves the Word of God and has been teaching through the Bible chapter by chapter for the better part of 40 years. By God's grace, He has allowed me to learn a thing or two along the way, but I remain a very fallible human being who is quite capable of forgetting or misstating some important truth from God's Word. For that reason, I encourage the readers of this book to study the Bible for themselves and test everything by the revelation of God's Word.

It is my humble prayer that this volume would be a blessing to those who are pressing into Jesus to seek a greater understanding of His glorious Word.

Pastor Paul LeBoutillier
July 2023

Chapter 1

SALVATION

- What happens to people who lived a good life but never heard the Gospel? 3

- How can God fairly judge us for our sin if we are born sinners? 5

- At what age can a person accept Christ? 7

- Can Christians lose their salvation? 8

- I was always told that if you sin after accepting Jesus you will lose your salvation. Is that true? 11

- Are some people predestined for hell? 12

- Are we saved by a choice of our own free will, or does God make that choice ahead of time? 14

- Will God send people to hell simply for not acknowledging Him? 16

- What does it mean to "work out your own salvation"? 18

- Will a person who has accepted Jesus still go to heaven if they were to take their own life? 19

2   PASTOR, I HAVE A QUESTION

- How were people saved before the time of Christ? 20

- Is water baptism a requirement for salvation? 21

- Should small children be baptized? 25

- Is it true that I can't go to heaven if I haven't received the baptism of the Holy Spirit? 27

What happens to people who lived a good life but never heard the Gospel?

Your question includes two assumptions: The first is that people are capable of a level of goodness that God, if He's truly *fair*, ought to recognize and reward with eternal life. And the second is that God is actually *unfair* and ignores human goodness, choosing instead to judge people on terms which may or may not be in our favor, that is, whether a person actually heard the Gospel.

Obviously, *both* of these assumptions are false and yet they remain challenging ideas, nonetheless. But the Bible makes it clear that people are *not* capable of a goodness that could ever earn us a place in heaven and that God also declares Himself perfectly fair and just with all His judgements.

Let me share with you some insights from God's Word that I believe will lead us to some satisfactory conclusions:

1. God wants us to be saved.
Through the inspiration of the Holy Spirit, the Apostle Peter wrote a wonderfully comforting statement in his second letter that goes like this:

The Lord is not slow in keeping his promise, as some understand slowness. He is patient with you, not wanting anyone to perish, but everyone to come to repentance. (2 Peter 3:9 NIV)

We can rest in the knowledge that God wants everyone to come to repentance and faith in His Son. That doesn't mean everyone will come to Christ, but it *does* mean God desires us to be saved.

4   PASTOR, I HAVE A QUESTION

2. God comes to us.

The book of Acts gives us some amazing accounts of God pulling out all the stops to bring the good news to people who had a heart to receive. One account tells of an Ethiopian eunuch and the other of a Roman Centurion, but in each case the Lord orchestrated circumstances in such a way that the Gospel *came* to them. This is the heart of God toward mankind — that He will do whatever needs to be done to bring people to the place of salvation. The bottom line is that God is *not* limited in how the Gospel gets to people.

3. God will do right.

Abraham faced some challenging questions similar to the one you're dealing with, specifically when it came to God's judgment upon a couple of cities where his nephew happened to be living. God revealed that He was about to destroy those places due to their wickedness, so Abraham began to pepper God with questions about His fairness. He ended with this amazing question: "**Will not the Judge of all the earth do right?**" (Genesis 18:25 NIV). That wasn't so much a question as it was a declaration of faith in God's justice — as if to say, "It is impossible for you to do anything except that which is entirely good and correct."

4. God has revealed Himself in Creation.

In Romans 1, the Apostle Paul writes about the revelation of God in Creation and how, because of that, people "are without excuse" (v. 20). It would seem from this passage that even in those areas where the Gospel has never been taken, God still has a means of determining a person's ultimate heart condition. How that judgment plays out and how the Lord completes people's understanding of forgiveness through Christ, we are not told. But there is enough information in those verses to help us understand that God is not without options.

The preaching of the Gospel appears to be God's primary means of disseminating the message of the cross to people. But whenever or wherever that option isn't available, our God continues to possess unlimited means to bring people to faith in Christ. Even when we're unaware of God's hidden methods, we continue to trust His character and amazing love.

How can God fairly judge us for our sin if we are born sinners?

What you're primarily asking is this: "**How is it fair that God holds us accountable for a sinful nature that was imposed upon us by someone else?**"

I'll admit at the outset that this is a very challenging question and one that I've grappled with over the years. Whatever I offer as a response probably wouldn't satisfy because we are simply told that Adam was our representative in the Garden and that his failure and the curse that attended it was passed along to us who are his descendants.

But obsessing over whether this was fair or not ignores any kind of acknowledgment of what God did to rectify the situation created by sin. He made a *free* way for us to avoid all judgment by taking that judgment upon Himself in the Person of His Son. This way is now ours if we turn from our sin and embrace His Son as Savior. He does not require us to be "good people" in order to clear us from accusation and judgment.

6 PASTOR, I HAVE A QUESTION

When people object to being saddled with a sinful nature they never chose, what they're *really* against is having to humble themselves and accept God's solution. To do that they would have to admit that they are sinners and are therefore separated from God; they are helpless in and of themselves to solve the problem; and accepting the death of Jesus is the only way for them to be saved. Some people find these things offensive, that they would rather just accuse God for allowing them to be born into sin, but all the while they are ignoring the incredible solution God offers to all mankind.

As the Apostle Paul wrote in Romans 5:19:

For just as through the disobedience of the one man [Adam] the many were made sinners, so also through the obedience of the one man [Jesus] the many will be made righteous. (NIV)

To summarize, I'll confess that I'm not totally certain about the ins and outs of Adam's original sin and the fairness of it getting passed along to us. But here's what I *do* know: Even though we're born sinful and separated from God, our Lord loved us *so much* that He made a way for our sins to be forgiven. And He Himself bore the full cost of that forgiveness. Do we really want to allow our lack of understanding in one area keep us from accepting God's love and forgiveness?

At what age can a person accept Christ?

There is nothing in Scripture that speaks of a specific age requirement for a person to receive Christ as Lord. And since Jesus exhorted us to receive the Kingdom "like a child" (Luke 18:17), I assume the decision of a child to embrace Christ is no less meaningful than that of an adult.

I don't think there's anything wrong with explaining the basics of Christ's love and sacrifice to a child and even encouraging them to ask Jesus to live in their heart. But as children begin to approach adulthood themselves, there will come a need one day for them to transfer their faith from the realm of their parent's supervision into a more mature understanding of their own personal need for Christ.

Over the years I've spoken to many adults who have shared how as children they opened their hearts to the Gospel, prayed the sinner's prayer, but later in life managed to walk away from following Christ out of neglect or a fascination with the world. In such cases, it's not uncommon for them to relate how they had little or no understanding of spiritual truths because they were never properly trained in the Word of God. As much as it pains me to say it, as often as there is a child praying to receive Christ as Savior, there is also an adult in that child's life thinking that nothing more is needed since the child has already made a decision for Christ.

Regardless of the age a child comes to Christ, there is always the need for discipleship and instruction in the Word. In many ways, a parent's job is just beginning when their child prays to receive the Lord.

Can Christians lose their salvation?

This is not a typical yes-or-no question. People deserve a thoughtful answer so I'm going to share and respond to what I have found to be the real concerns that lurk *behind* this question.

Here's the first version of what some people are actually asking: "**If I continue to make mistakes and fall into sin, is there a point where God will say, 'That's enough!' and erase my name from the Book of Life?**"

The answer is *no*. I do not believe it is possible to lose your salvation because of sin. You didn't receive salvation because of your goodness, so how in the world could you lose it due to sin?

The fact that this question even exists suggests a lack of understanding of what Jesus did on the cross. Sin has been dealt with once and for all for those who come to the cross by faith and receive the sacrifice of Jesus Christ. When Jesus said "It is finished," He meant that sin was paid for *completely* by His suffering and death. To suggest that a believer's sin could somehow nullify that suffering is, to be quite honest, absurd.

Finally, if salvation could be lost due to sin, it would mean that we are saved by grace but *kept* in a place of salvation by our own goodness which in the end simply equates to salvation by works.

Although failures are inevitable, God's grace is greater still and the blood of Jesus Christ keeps on cleansing us from sin (see 1 John 1:7).

The second variation of this question goes like this: "**If I**

commit some sin and fail to confess it before I die, will God send me to hell?"

This question is closely related to the one we just looked at, and it comes from those who believe they must keep themselves saved by confessing and repenting of any and all sin. Although it's a popular belief among far too many Christians, once again it's just a thinly veiled version of salvation by works.

We are saved by placing our confidence in the finished work of Jesus Christ on the cross — not by flawlessly confessing each and every sin we've ever committed.

The third version of this question is a more straightforward one that wants to know: **"Is it possible for a born-again believer to go from faith to unbelief?"**

There are many in the Body of Christ who would respond to this question with a resounding "NO!" This seems to be the belief upheld by the majority. My only problem with that response is that it flies in the face of God's Word.

I find the New Testament filled with repeated warnings written to born-again believers about the danger of abandoning faith and walking away from Christ. (And by walking away from Christ, I am not talking about committing sin. Again, believers cannot lose their salvation by sinning any more than they can earn eternal life by doing good.)

If walking away from the Lord in unbelief isn't possible as many believe and teach, I have to ask myself why there are so many warnings like the ones below scattered throughout the New Testament:

Now I would remind you, brothers, of the gospel I preached to you, which you received, in which you stand, and by which you

10   PASTOR, I HAVE A QUESTION

*are being saved, **if** you hold fast to the word I preached to you — unless you believed in vain.* (1 Corinthians 15:1–2)

I highlighted the word "if" because it introduces a conditional clause. (A lot of Christians forget that although salvation is free, it is *not* unconditional. It is conditioned on faith.) As the Apostle Paul states above, the continuation of faith is also necessary. Furthermore, we can also see from the passage above that Paul believed it was possible to "believe in vain."

Also, take note of the Apostle's words in Galatians 5:

Look: I, Paul, say to you that if you accept circumcision, Christ will be of no advantage to you. I testify again to every man who accepts circumcision that he is obligated to keep the whole law. You are severed from Christ, you who would be justified by the law; you have fallen away from grace. (vv. 2–4)

The Apostle Paul believed that it was possible to "fall away from grace." But how? In this case it was by adding circumcision as a requirement for salvation. This is what the believers in the Galatian churches were doing and Paul warned them that if they made that move, "Christ will be of no advantage" to them. Take note that this warning was spoken to believers.

Finally, we see that the author of Hebrews believed it was possible to "drift away" from the message of faith in Jesus Christ.

Therefore we must pay much closer attention to what we have heard, lest we drift away from it. For since the message declared by angels proved to be reliable, and every transgression or disobedience received a just retribution, how shall we escape if we neglect such a great salvation? (Hebrews 2:1–3a)

I understand there are many sincere followers of Christ who passionately reject any idea of a true believer walking away from the Lord in unbelief. I respect their position, but as I study the Word of God, I cannot embrace it because of repeated warnings by New Testament authors about doing that very thing. As a Bible teacher, it is my responsibility to respectfully communicate the message of God's Word without bias or partiality. Although it seems impossible to imagine someone being saved and later being unsaved, each and every believer must ultimately allow the Word to have the final say on how they view this issue.

So, can you lose your salvation due to sin? Heavens, no! The Apostle Paul told us that nothing can separate us from the love of God in Jesus Christ our Lord (see Romans 8).

Can a believer eventually adopt a position of unbelief and walk away from the Lord? The Bible suggests that is possible.

I was always told that if you sin after accepting Jesus you will lose your salvation. Is that true?

This is all too common. Essentially the message is: Jesus died to save you from your sin, but once you accept His sacrifice on the cross you need to stop sinning to *stay* saved. But the Bible teaches that our salvation is a gift from God and the forgiveness we are granted through Jesus is ongoing — even when we sin.

One of the most wonderful promises from God's Word is found in 1 John 1:7 which says, "**But if we walk in the light, as he is in the light, we have fellowship with one another, and the blood of Jesus, his Son, purifies us from all sin.**"

The verb "purifies" is in the present tense in the Greek and it speaks of an ongoing provision of forgiveness against present and future sins. It could literally be translated this way: "and the blood of Jesus, his Son, *keeps on cleansing* us from all sin."

God knows that we are sinful and imperfect, and He made a way for the sacrifice of His Son to keep pouring out His mercy on our lives.

Are some people predestined for hell?

Predestined means to be predetermined by God to either be saved or lost. The evidence of Scripture tells us that the answer to this question is no — God does *not* predestine people to hell. Consider the following passages and the conclusion drawn from each statement:

This is good, and it is pleasing in the sight of God our Savior, who desires all people to be saved and to come to the knowledge of the truth. (1 Timothy 2:3–4)

Conclusion: If God predestined some for hell, this statement could not be true.

For God so loved the world, that he gave his only Son, that whoever believes in him should not perish but have eternal life. (John 3:16)

Conclusion: If God predestined some for hell, eternal life would *not* be open to "whoever," and this statement would not be true.

SALVATION   13

The Lord is not slow to fulfill his promise as some count slowness, but is patient toward you, not wishing that any should perish, but that all should reach repentance. (2 Peter 3:9)

Conclusion: It is a contradiction to say that God predestines people to hell and at the same time wishes none to perish.

He is the atoning sacrifice for our sins, and not only for ours but also for the sins of the whole world. (1 John 2:2 NIV)

Conclusion: This passage clearly tells us that Jesus died "for the sins of the whole world." That means salvation is extended (available) to everyone.

Regarding predestination, the Bible says: "**For those whom he foreknew he also predestined to be conformed to the image of his Son, in order that he might be the firstborn among many brothers**" (Romans 8:29).

Notice in this passage that predestination concerns those who are saved and *not* those who are lost. And even in the case of the saved, predestination is according to the foreknowledge of God. In other words, God, being outside of time, knows all things before they happen (foreknowledge). He therefore knows who would come to Christ, and He also predestined them to be conformed into the image of His Son.

Some who believe that God predestined some to be lost and spend eternity in hell cite Romans 9:22 which says: "**What if God, desiring to show his wrath and to make known his power, has endured with much patience vessels of wrath prepared for destruction...**"

This verse is often quoted as a proof text to support the idea that some people are really predestined to hell. But note that the phrase "vessels of wrath prepared for destruction" refers to those whose own determination to sin make them

14   PASTOR, I HAVE A QUESTION

objects of God's righteous wrath. They are then "prepared for destruction" by their own sin and rejection of Christ — not by a decree of God that sentences them to hell before they were ever born.

Are we saved by a choice of our own free will, or does God make that choice ahead of time?

This question represents a classic area of disagreement between Christians. There are two schools of thought and each holds tenaciously to their position. One says that every individual is personally responsible for their decision to make Christ Savior and Lord and that their status as a born-again Christian is *entirely* one of their own free will. The other side holds just as firmly to the belief that we are chosen beforehand through the sovereignty of God and are predestined to be saved. They would say any "choice" we have in the matter is simply because we were chosen first by God.

The solution to this conundrum, which seems to completely escape proponents of both sides, is one that does no violence to the body of Scripture. Simply put, *both* positions are equally true. I am aware that there are many who believe what I have just said to be patently impossible. They themselves are unable to reconcile how salvation can be the result of both an act of their free will and God's predestination at the same time. Therefore, they reject this conclusion out of hand. But I would argue for its validity from two perspectives:

1. It is biblical.
There's no question that the Bible speaks of God's sovereign election (predestination) of the saints. Romans 8 is one very clear example. In a similar fashion, there are also passages of Scripture which speak of the choice given to mankind. The King James Version renders Revelation 22:17 this way: "And whosoever will, let him take the water of life freely." The NIV (1984) uses the words "whoever wishes" and the NKJV says "whoever desires." The idea is clearly set forth that there *is* a choice we face in receiving Christ as Lord and is repeated many times throughout the Word of God.

2. Reconciling these two ideas is not our responsibility.
Christians often fall into the trap of accepting or rejecting a truth based on whether they can personally comprehend it. Holding to such an idea may require you to take a scissors to your Bible and "cherry-pick" the truths you find convenient or those you can easily understand. Can you comprehend eternity? How about the Trinity? Yet these truths are clearly revealed in God's Word.

At the end of the day, my responsibility is to prayerfully look into the Word of God and determine what truth it reveals, regardless of whether I can personally explain them from an intellectual standpoint. When all is said and done, what we will ultimately be able to lay hold of are the things that the Bible *does* reveal about our salvation: that God elected us for salvation according to His foreknowledge, and that we must choose (receive) Christ according to the gift of our free will. As for explaining how those two realities can coexist, that's God's business, not mine.

Will God send people to hell simply for not acknowledging Him?

This is a perfect example of how easy it is to make God sound like a monster just by cunningly wording a question.

For starters, *no one* winds up in hell simply for failing to acknowledge God. (Even Christians fail to acknowledge God sometimes.) Hell will be populated by people who vehemently reject God — those who say, "I want nothing to do with God or His Son. I refuse to turn from my sin, and I reject everything associated with God."

Secondly, you need to understand that hell is *never* God's intended destination for anyone! In fact, we're told that hell was originally created for the devil, not for man. The Scripture clearly says that God is "not wanting anyone to perish, but everyone to come to repentance" (2 Peter 3:9 NIV). People have to literally *choose* hell over God's offer of forgiveness through Jesus Christ.

Jesus laid down His life for sinners. He suffered terribly on the cross, bearing the condemnation that we deserved. He didn't *have* to do any of that. But when He did, He made forgiveness freely available to *anyone* who would humble themselves and receive Him as Savior. To reject that free gift of forgiveness is to throw away any chance of being saved. Why? Because, as Jesus said, "I am the way, and the truth, and the life. No one comes to the Father except through me" (John 14:6).

It is only by *rejecting* the work of Christ and what He accomplished for us on the cross that people put themselves in danger of hell. The word *reject* also means "to refuse to accept." Some synonyms include: *decline*, *deny*, and *disapprove*

SALVATION   17

— words which practically mean "to refuse to believe" and "to declare something as untrue." Hell, therefore, will be made up of those who have rejected God's free gift of life.

The follow-up question to this one is: **"What about those who have never heard about Jesus or God's love?"** The answer to that question comes in two parts. The first comes from Romans 1 which says of God:

For his invisible attributes, namely, his eternal power and divine nature, have been clearly perceived, ever since the creation of the world, in the things that have been made. So they are without excuse. (v. 20)

God has revealed Himself in all that He has created. Even if people have never heard of God, there is a judgment based solely on a person's response to all that they can see in this world and beyond. Creation infers that there *is* a Creator behind it all. This evidence in creation is so profound that the Apostle Paul said that men are "without excuse" as to their determination of God's existence.

The second part of this answer is given to us in a fascinating conversation between Abraham and God. When Abraham was told by the Lord that Sodom and Gomorrah were about to be judged for their sin, Abraham began to fear for his nephew who lived among the wicked people of those cities. He finally asked the Lord, **"Will not the Judge of all the earth do right?"** (Genesis 18:25 NIV).

When we ask questions such as, "How will God deal with those who have never heard the Gospel?"— we are essentially asking this very question: *"Will not the Judge of all the earth do right?"* And the answer is yes! He will! Since God is perfect in all His ways, that means His judgments will be unblemished and without error, His compassion absolute and untainted, and His love perfect and unselfish.

God makes no errors. On the day that men stand before the justice of God's eternal holiness, there will be no allegations of unfairness or injustice on God's part. All things will be done in the perfection of His character.

What does it mean to "work out your own salvation"?

Let's look at the actual passage from God's Word:

Therefore, my beloved, as you have always obeyed, so now, not only as in my presence but much more in my absence, work out your own salvation with fear and trembling, for it is God who works in you, both to will and to work for his good pleasure. (Philippians 2:12–13)

Working *out* one's salvation does not mean working *for* salvation. Rather, it speaks of making salvation functional in all areas of life. It speaks of inviting Jesus to be Lord in more and more areas of everyday living.

The moment we come to Christ is only the beginning of our walk with the Lord. From there, the Holy Spirit encourages us to go deeper into the life of Christ — as far as we are willing to go. To do this He speaks to us about new and different areas where we can surrender control to His lordship. Our marriage, our work, our daily speech, and even our thoughts — nothing is off-limits. And as we concede more and more of these areas of our lives and turn them over to Jesus, we are said to be working (i.e., walking) out our own salvation.

So, think of Philippians 2:12-13 as an exhortation to go deeper into Christ, and with a surrendered heart allow Him to exercise His rule and reign over all the areas of your life.

Will a person who has accepted Jesus still go to heaven if they were to take their own life?

Whenever a question such as this one comes up, I feel it is important to ask the real question behind it. In other words, what we're *really* asking here is, does the act of taking one's own life nullify a person's faith in the sacrifice of Jesus Christ on the cross? And, for that matter, are there *any actions* on our part that can overturn or cancel our salvation? Once we determine the answer to these questions, all the others will fall into place.

From a purely biblical standpoint I would have to say that no action, deed, or misstep on our part has the power to cancel out or invalidate what Christ has accomplished for us on the cross. Since Ephesians 2:8-9 makes it clear that we did nothing good to merit salvation, it makes sense to conclude that we can do nothing bad to spoil it.

Some people claim that suicide is proof that an individual never had saving faith in the first place, but such a statement lacks foundation. Nothing in the Bible supports that conclusion.

All that being said, I must say that suicide is the ultimate act of placing one's own will above the will of God. A large part of coming to Christ is learning to daily surrender one's

20 PASTOR, I HAVE A QUESTION

life to His lordship. That involves bending our will to His and even accepting suffering if that is God's plan. Peter wrote, "**Therefore let those who suffer according to God's will entrust their souls to a faithful Creator while doing good**" (1 Peter 4:19).

How were people saved before the time of Christ?

We know that Jesus came to die on the cross bearing the penalty of our sin. We also know that the death of Christ happened at a specific point in time. Many Christians wonder how those who lived *before* the time of Christ were saved or if eternal life for them was a possibility.

There are many who believe that before the time of Christ, people were saved by keeping the Law. However, if you carefully read the Old Testament, you'll find that among the promises outlined for obedience there was never a promise of heaven. This is confirmed in the New Testament in passages such as Romans 3:20 which says, "Therefore no one will be declared righteous in God's sight by the works of the law" (NIV).

In Ephesians 2:8–9, the Apostle Paul reminds us that we are saved *by grace through faith*. He says that salvation is not a work of our own effort or merit but is instead "the gift of God." Although this is what we refer to as the Gospel (which means *good news*), there is no reason to believe that the way of salvation has ever been different. Faith in God has always been the key.

As far back as Genesis 15, we're told that Abraham believed the LORD, and God "credited it to him as righteousness" (Genesis 15:6 NIV). And in the Psalms, we see that God had always been communicating to His people, "Blessed are all who take refuge in him" (Psalm 2:12).

People who lived and died before Christ had to trust God and rely on His mercy just like we do. Their faith looked forward to Christ's work on the cross, while ours looks backward. I'm not suggesting they had the full picture of God's redemptive program — not by a long shot. Their faith was based on the amount of revelation they had been given.

The important thing to remember is that there has never been a different way to be saved other than placing one's faith completely in God's mercy.

Is water baptism a requirement for salvation?

For many years people have debated whether water baptism is a requirement for salvation. One passage used to support this belief is Acts 2:38.

And Peter said to them, "Repent and be baptized every one of you in the name of Jesus Christ for the forgiveness of your sins, and you will receive the gift of the Holy Spirit."

Proponents of such a belief would say that God has established a biblical formula for salvation. That process goes like this:

22   PASTOR, I HAVE A QUESTION

1. Repent.

2. Be baptized.

3. Receive forgiveness.

4. Receive the Holy Spirit.

At least that's the way it's laid out in Acts 2:38, right?

I will wholeheartedly agree that water baptism is closely tied with salvation in the New Testament, but the question still remains: *Is it required?* In other words, if someone was dying and prayed to receive Christ, but passed away just moments later — would that person be refused acceptance into God's presence on the basis of not having been baptized in water?

Here are four reasons why I believe water baptism is important, but *not* a requirement for salvation.

Reason 1: The Formula Turned Upside-down
Those who believe that baptism is a requirement to be saved love to cite the verse quoted above (Acts 2:38), believing that it reveals a formula for how a person is saved.

The only problem is that the formula is reversed a little later on in the book of Acts. In chapter 10 when Peter goes to the home of a Roman centurion, we see that the people believed and received the Holy Spirit *before* getting baptized in water. The passage goes like this:

While Peter was still saying these things, the Holy Spirit fell on all who heard the word. And the believers from among the circumcised who had come with Peter were amazed, because the gift of the Holy Spirit was poured out even on the Gentiles. For they were hearing them speaking in tongues and extolling God. Then Peter declared, "Can anyone withhold water for baptizing

these people, who have received the Holy Spirit just as we have?"
And he commanded them to be baptized in the name of Jesus
Christ. Then they asked him to remain for some days. (Acts
10:44–48)

Notice the order in this passage: faith, receiving the Holy
Spirit, then baptism. Telling people they must be baptized
before they can be saved finds a biblical roadblock here.

Reason 2: The Testimony of Scripture
There are several passages in the New Testament that speak
of how a person is saved, and most of them make no mention
of water baptism. Here are just a few:

And it shall come to pass that everyone who calls upon the name
of the Lord shall be saved. (Acts 2:21)

...if you confess with your mouth that Jesus is Lord and believe
in your heart that God raised him from the dead, you will be
saved. For with the heart one believes and is justified, and with
the mouth one confesses and is saved. (Romans 10:9–10)

For God so loved the world, that he gave his only Son, that
whoever believes in him should not perish but have eternal life.
(John 3:16)

Reason 3: The Testimony of the Apostle Paul
Here is Paul's statement to the Corinthian church where he
declares that God did not call him to baptize:

For Christ did not send me to baptize but to preach the gospel,
and not with words of eloquent wisdom, lest the cross of Christ
be emptied of its power. (1 Corinthians 1:17)

In this chapter, Paul thanks God that he didn't baptize most
of the people of Corinth (1:14). Would the Apostle make such
a reckless statement if baptism were required for salvation?

24 PASTOR, I HAVE A QUESTION

Reason 4: The Testimony of Grace

The most important statement securing our belief that water baptism is not a requirement for salvation is Ephesians 2:8–9 which says:

For by grace you have been saved through faith. And this is not your own doing; it is the gift of God, not a result of works, so that no one may boast.

The Apostle Paul reminds us in this passage that our salvation is not our own doing. It is entirely a gift, by grace through faith. Grace means "without merit" — apart from anything we might otherwise do to earn that salvation. The fact remains that to *require* water baptism is to demand an act that the recipient must *perform* before salvation is bestowed. That takes the gift of eternal life out of the realm of grace, and firmly into the realm of works.

The salvation given us through Jesus Christ removes all boasting. Nothing of my own doing has helped to secure my salvation. Nothing.

So, should a believer be baptized in water? Absolutely! Not *for* salvation, but *because of* salvation. The waters of baptism are a beautiful, public declaration of our faith in Jesus and our identification with Him in His death, burial, and resurrection.

Should small children be baptized?

This question is one I have agonized over for the most of my time as a pastor — not because the Bible is ambiguous on the subject, but because there's never a shortage of parents wanting to see their children baptized. I can't blame them for that, but many times I find myself in the position of having to speak with the parents and explain to them that water baptism does *not* guarantee one's salvation. I know of several instances when parents rushed their children into being baptized for the wrong reasons and this often brought about confusion later on. My own parents had me baptized as an infant although I'm not certain what they really believed it accomplished.

A little background may be helpful. In the early 5th century A.D., a man named Augustine rose to prominence in the church and became bishop of Hippo in North Africa. Augustine was brilliant and his writings are still studied today, but some of what he believed weren't thoroughly biblical. Regarding water baptism, for example, Augustine believed that all who receive water baptism become recipients of a regenerating grace. This belief was passed along to the Roman Catholic Church and continues to be a popular idea today. It's a lovely thought — the only problem is that this idea is nowhere found in Scripture. Even so, there are still many people today who are stuck in the mindset that baptism guarantees one's future salvation and because of this, they wish to see their children baptized.

Water Baptism is only ever portrayed in God's Word as an act of obedience on the part of those who have already come to faith in Jesus as Savior. The act itself of being baptized is a declaration of one's identification with Jesus in His death, burial, and resurrection — all depicted beautifully

26   PASTOR, I HAVE A QUESTION

as the new believer is immersed into the waters of baptism (signifying our identification with Christ in His death) and then immediately raised again (indicating our identification with Jesus in His resurrection).

While I completely agree that children can fully know and understand the Gospel and truly be born again, I do not agree that they can fully grasp the idea of water baptism in terms of what it represents. This is because the idea of entering into Jesus' death (which is depicted in water baptism) speaks to the issue of dying to self and recognizing that we are now called to choose Jesus over the life of the flesh that wars against the life of the Spirit. And having died to self, water baptism goes on to symbolize the reality of being raised to new life through the power of the Spirit. The life of the Spirit and the life of the flesh are concepts that small children are likely to find very difficult to grasp, but I believe they are essential for making our motivation for being baptized in water truly biblical.

My wife and I raised four kids of our own and I have to tell you, I wish I had encouraged them to wait until they were older and better able to understand what they were doing. I believe I robbed them of what could have been a more meaningful and genuine expression of their faith by allowing them to be baptized when they were younger.

So, what age is best? That's hard to say because children grow and mature at different levels. When a child comes to the place of understanding the life of the flesh versus the life of the Spirit and how believers are called to die to self and live to Christ — they are ready to express that understanding in the waters of baptism. Until then, the very last thing we want to do in a child's life is to leave them with the impression that they were baptized in water and as a result, everything concerning heaven is settled. We are *not* saved by being baptized in water. Instead, we are saved by placing our faith in the finished work of Jesus Christ on the cross.

Is it true that I can't go to heaven if I haven't received the baptism of the Holy Spirit?

The Bible makes it clear that salvation is obtained by placing our faith in the finished work of Jesus Christ on the cross for the forgiveness of our sins (see John 1:12–13; Romans 10:9; Ephesians 2:8–9). Jesus paid *in full* the penalty of our sin, and what this means for us is that by placing our faith in his death on our behalf, we are saved from bearing our own penalty. When Jesus uttered the words "It is finished" from the cross, He was declaring that the penalty of our sin was paid in full. When we accept *by faith* that He accomplished all this for us, the Bible declares that our sins are blotted out and we are made children of God.

The baptism of the Holy Spirit comes into view *after* salvation. It is designed to *empower* believers for service, not to save them.

Chapter 2

OUR STRUGGLE WITH SIN

- If I'm saved and my sins are forgiven, why then is it important to sin no more? 29

- If I am set free from sin, why do I still sin? 31

- How can I break free from a cycle of sin? 33

- What is the biblical antidote for pride and how can we apply it? 36

If I'm saved and my sins are forgiven, why then is it important to sin no more?

This is an excellent question, and the Bible has no shortage of answers. So, why should a believer be concerned with curbing sin if forgiveness and eternal salvation are secured through faith in Christ? I will give you seven reasons:

1. A life of sin is incompatible with the life of the Holy Spirit now indwelling us.

For the sinful nature desires what is contrary to the Spirit, and the Spirit what is contrary to the sinful nature. They are in conflict with each other... (Galatians 5:17 NIV84)

Believers who yield to a life of sin will be in constant conflict with and under steady conviction of the Holy Spirit who now indwells them. In a word, they will be miserable. (See Psalm 32:3–4 to see how David described this kind of conviction.)

2. Although it can be a difficult concept to grasp, the Bible says we have "died to sin."

The Apostle Paul wrote:

What shall we say, then? Shall we go on sinning so that grace may increase? By no means! We died to sin; how can we live in it any longer? (Romans 6:1–2 NIV84)

When we come to Christ as Savior, we literally enter into His death. That means we are now dead to the control of the old sinful nature that once dominated our behavior and are now free to follow Christ and make Him Lord of our lives. To live in sin would be a complete denial of the freedom Christ won for us on the cross. Living in sin means walking back into a life of slavery and bondage to the flesh.

30   PASTOR, I HAVE A QUESTION

3. Victory over sin is the sign that we have come to know Him and are born of Him.

We know that we have come to know him if we obey his commands. (1 John 2:3 NIV84)

Also check out 1 John 2:29; 3:6 and 5:18.

4. The renewing of our mind enables us to test and approve God's will.

Do not conform any longer to the pattern of this world, but be transformed by the renewing of your mind. Then you will be able to test and approve what God's will is — his good, pleasing and perfect will. (Romans 12:2 NIV84)

5. We owe Jesus our obedience, gratitude, and worship.

Therefore, I urge you, brothers, in view of God's mercy, to offer your bodies as living sacrifices, holy and pleasing to God — this is your spiritual act of worship. (Romans 12:1 NIV 84)

6. Sin always brings death.

Don't be lulled into the idea that just because you're a Christian, sin can no longer produce death in your life. I have personally witnessed born-again believers suffer great loss because they carelessly allowed sin to increase in their lives. Everything from the death of a marriage, the loss of a family, or the diminishing of a career can easily develop from a life of reckless ignorance.

For the wages of sin is death... (Romans 6:23)

...after desire has conceived, it gives birth to sin; and sin, when it is full-grown, gives birth to death. (James 1:15 NIV)

And finally...

7. Because of sin, the wrath of God is coming.

Put to death, therefore, whatever belongs to your earthly nature: sexual immorality, impurity, lust, evil desires and greed, which is idolatry. Because of these, the wrath of God is coming. (Colossians 3:5–6 NIV)

The acts of the sinful nature are obvious: sexual immorality, impurity and debauchery; idolatry and witchcraft; hatred, discord, jealousy, fits of rage, selfish ambition, dissensions, factions and envy; drunkenness, orgies, and the like. I warn you, as I did before, that those who live like this will not inherit the kingdom of God. (Galatians 5:19–21 NIV84)

All in all, I think these biblical reasons for avoiding sin are compelling. Obviously, I could have come up with many more witnesses from God's Word, but I think the point has been sufficiently made. As a new creation in Christ, a life of sin no longer fits with our eternal destiny and blessing. In fact, it's the opposite of what God wants to do in our hearts.

If I am set free from sin, why do I still sin?

Born-again Christians still sin for lots of reasons. In some cases, it's because we've established deep ruts of habitual behavior that are challenging to break out of. Other times it's because we simply choose to disobey God. Then there are also times when we fail to discern dangerous circumstances until it's too late.

One of the benefits of being born-again is that Jesus sets us free from the dominion of our sinful nature. That means we now have the freedom to say no to the voice of temptation and resist the impulse to sin. We didn't have that freedom before we came to Christ. At that time, we were slaves to sin and in bondage to our sinful nature. But since coming to Jesus, we've been set free to choose the leading of God's Holy Spirit instead of running after the desires of our flesh.

That said, you must understand that the very freedom you've been given means you are completely free — free to choose to do right or do wrong. (That's what real freedom is: the ability to go whichever way you wish.) And the fact is, sometimes we choose to go God's way and sometimes we choose to follow the impulses of our flesh and fall back into sin. But there's good news. The blood that Jesus shed for you and me on the cross is a perpetual source of forgiveness, even when we fail to follow the leading of the Spirit as we should. As the Apostle John wrote:

I am writing these things to you so that you may not sin. But if anyone does sin, we have an advocate with the Father, Jesus Christ the righteous. (1 John 2:1)

We've been given the living Word to keep us from sin. However, when we do sin, John says that we have an advocate with the Father. The word advocate means "one who pleads the cause of another." This doesn't mean we take sinning lightly. On the contrary, we understand from God's Word that sin still has painful consequences, even for those who are saved. But even so, we know that the failings of our flesh can never tear us away from the love of Jesus Christ. His hold on us is stronger than our sin.

So what can you and I do to keep ourselves from falling into sin? We need to stay in the Word and stay connected to other believers. (We were never meant to be Christians on our own.) We also need to pray about the weak areas of our flesh and memorize Bible passages that speak directly to those areas. We constantly have to ask God to give us the strength that will enable us to overcome the downward pull of our flesh and stand strong against the temptations of the enemy and this world.

All believers struggle with sin. It's part of what it means to be a born-again Christian. And you will continue to struggle with sin until the day you are released from your body of flesh. But there is hope. You just need to realize that the power to overcome sin does not come from you. Instead, it is found in Jesus Christ and it is activated by faith.

How can I break free from a cycle of sin?

The Apostle Paul wrote, **"it is God who works in you, both to will and to work for his good pleasure"** (Philippians 2:13). Your desire to be free from the cycle of sin tells me that God has already given you the will to do His good pleasure. You're just stumbling in the area of carrying it out.

You must understand that sin creates *very deep ruts* in our lives (the world calls them "addictions") and breaking free from those ruts is extremely challenging. It takes dedication and faith. Let me share some suggestions as well as some pitfalls that you will want to avoid:

1. Do not doubt your salvation. Doubt is one of Satan's most effective tools to bring discouragement to the child of God. Struggling with sin is not a sign that you are unsaved. In

34   PASTOR, I HAVE A QUESTION

fact, quite the opposite. Before a person comes to Christ, they don't struggle with sin. They just do it. But once we come to Jesus by faith, His Spirit works conviction and understanding about our sinful behaviors and that is when the struggle truly begins.

2. Do not doubt God's love for you or His willingness to help you. One of the biggest pitfalls for those struggling with some besetting sin is the temptation to become overly introspective. They examine their every thought and motive as well as God's attitudes and motives and conclude: "*Maybe God doesn't want to help me,*" or "*Maybe my sin is punishment for my past,*" or "*Maybe God has given me over to my sin and there's no hope for me.*" Those who give into such thoughts eventually fall into a maze of confusing and errant notions that bear no resemblance to the truth. It only breeds discouragement. Don't go there!

3. Do NOT focus on self-effort. You cannot break free from this cycle of sin on your own. It simply isn't possible. You need to come to the Lord daily in prayer. Tell the Lord that you need Him to set you free and that you are waiting on Him to give you strength each day. The Apostle Paul wrote that we put no confidence in the flesh (Philippians 3:3). Tell the Lord that you place no confidence or hope in your own power to break free from your sin, but that your confidence and hope is entirely in Him.

4. Do NOT look to the world for answers. The world in which we live knows only the power of "self" so don't go looking there for answers. Keep your heart focused on the Lord and His Word. Expose your heart to the Word daily and make sure you're being spiritually nourished (see Psalm 119:11).

OUR STRUGGLE WITH SIN   35

5. Make no provision for the flesh. Romans 13:14 tells us to **"put on the Lord Jesus Christ, and make no provision for the flesh, to gratify its desires."** There's an old saying that goes like this: *If you don't want to fall off the cliff, don't play around the edge.* This means you need to be careful about needlessly placing yourself in the path of temptation. You also need to think about what things in your life may be perpetuating your sin. Are you watching movies or reading books that portray sexual acts, or is the Internet a constant temptation to go where you shouldn't go? Remember that Jesus told us to be radical in our dealings with sin (see Matthew 18:7–9). Sometimes we have to radically disconnect our lives from the things that cause us to fall into sin.

6. Take each day as it comes. If you're having trouble trusting God for the whole day, then pray for strength for the next hour. Literally set your watch on the hour and pray, *"Lord, I ask you for the strength to get through this next hour."* Then as you get stronger, pray for the morning, and then pray for the afternoon, and then pray for the evening. Then eventually pray for each day. Take it *slow.* Only take as much of your day as your faith allows.

7. Do not allow failure to deter you from pressing onward. Satan wants you to give up and he will highlight your failures to get you to feel discouraged and hopeless. Don't let your feelings rule your life. It's natural to feel bad when you mess up, but ultimately, you need to listen to God rather than your feelings and press on.

8. Pray for an accountability partner. Ask the Lord to bring a mature believer into your life that you can talk and pray with, but most of all, someone who will ask you the hard questions and hold you accountable.

9. Stay in the Word of God. It is through the Word that we build up and strengthen our faith (Romans 10:17). Remember: "**All Scripture is breathed out by God and profitable for teaching, for reproof, for correction, and for training in righteousness, that the man of God may be complete, equipped for every good work**" (2 Timothy 3:16–17). Spend time reading and meditating on the Scriptures every day. Memorize passages that speak to your specific issue and recite them often — especially when you're feeling weak.

10. Cry out to God. The Psalmist wrote, "**When the righteous cry for help, the LORD hears and delivers them out of all their troubles**" (Psalm 34:17). Believers are made righteous through the blood of Jesus Christ, so what remains for us is to cry out to the Lord with our whole heart. Don't give up! Stay on course. There is freedom at the end of this road.

What is the biblical antidote for pride and how can we apply it?

The remedy for pride is knowing the truth and believing it! All throughout Scripture I see the truth that I am born into sin and utterly helpless to do anything about it apart from the intervention of my Savior. Furthermore, any good thing or gift that I possess is from God and does not come from me. In fact, "nothing good dwells in me" (Romans 7:18). If that reality doesn't keep me grounded, nothing will.

Chapter 3

FORGIVING OTHERS

- How can I genuinely and completely forgive others? 38

- Does genuinely forgiving someone also mean letting that person back into my life? 40

- Are Christians required to forgive even when there is no repentance? 41

- What should I do when forgiveness is expressed but not really shown? 43

- What if a believer chooses not to forgive? 44

- Should a Christian refrain from taking anyone to court? 46

How can I genuinely and completely forgive others?

Forgiveness is an interesting dynamic. Some people are naturally inclined to forgive, while others refuse to forgive even the slightest offense. (Some even create offenses where none exist!) As Christians, we are called to forgive others. But let's face it, forgiveness doesn't always come easy, right? Here are some steps that might help:

Step One: Confess to God that you are completely incapable of forgiving on your own. This is an incredibly important first step. Saying "I can't do it, but You can" is tremendously freeing because we're placing the emphasis of ability squarely where it needs to be — on the Lord's power.

Step Two: When we come to God for help in forgiving others, we often end up receiving all kinds of insights about *ourselves*. The Lord faithfully uses our weakness to highlight our own limitations and heart condition. With His help, we come to realize that although we've truly been hurt, we're not entirely the victim. We need to be quick to bring these kinds of revelations to the cross and confess them as sin.

Step Three: Focus on how much God has forgiven YOU! This may seem like a strange step, but it's absolutely huge. The Apostle Paul wrote:

Bear with each other and forgive whatever grievances you may have against one another. Forgive as the Lord forgave you. (Colossians 3:13 NIV84)

Understanding the depth of our own sin against God is the backdrop of how God wants us to view the offenses of others toward us. In essence God is saying: *Look, I know this person hurt you, and I acknowledge that hurt. But you need to*

FORGIVING OTHERS 39

understand that the hurts you've suffered are nothing compared to the offenses you've committed against Me. I have forgiven you — completely. Now go and do likewise in the power of my Spirit.

Step Four: This one is another crucial step not to miss. Jesus said, "**But I tell you who hear me: Love your enemies, do good to those who hate you, bless those who curse you, pray for those who mistreat you**" (Luke 6:27–28 NIV84). Praying for people who have hurt and misused us is far more than just a good thing to do, it also sets us free! When someone hurts me, I begin to pray for them, asking for God's blessing in their life. At first, I don't want to do it and I would much rather ask God to pluck their eyes out, but that's my flesh talking. Over time it gets easier to say the words and then after a while something amazing happens — I find that as I'm praying for them, I actually *mean* what I'm praying. As I ask the Lord to pour out His heart and grace on that person, I find that I'm entirely genuine in my desires. It is then I realize that God has set me free from the resentment and bitterness of my own hurts.

A great passage to meditate on is this one:

See to it that no one misses the grace of God and that no bitter root grows up to cause trouble and defile many. (Hebrews 12:15 NIV84)

A bitter root is something to be avoided at all costs! It begins with hurt and then justifies itself along the way by remembering and rehearsing the depth of the hurt caused. But in the end, it only serves to poison the heart of the person who entertained it.

Does genuinely forgiving someone also mean letting that person back into my life?

There is a belief among many that **real** forgiveness is always automatically tied to giving the offending person another chance and allowing them back into one's life. This idea is so strong, even among Christians, that some believers will actually withhold forgiveness out of fear that if they do forgive, that means letting the offending person back into their lives and therefore, having those offenses repeated.

But is that true? Does your refusal to let someone back into your life prove that you haven't truly forgiven them?

There is a story recorded in 1 Samuel that gives some insight on this matter. Chapter 26 records the events of a time when David was on the run from King Saul because the king wanted David dead. However, when Saul came out to pursue David, the Lord created circumstances in which David had the advantage and the opportunity to kill Saul while he slept. But even with all this, David refused to take Saul's life.

When King Saul discovered that David had spared his life, the king openly and publicly expressed deep regret for his actions. Furthermore, he encouraged David to return home with promises that no harm would ever come to him. He said, "**I have sinned. Return, my son David, for I will no more do you harm, because my life was precious in your eyes this day. Behold, I have acted foolishly, and have made a great mistake**" (1 Samuel 26:21). But the chapter ends by saying that **David went his way, and Saul returned to his place** (v. 25b).

David chose to forgive Saul for all the evil and cruelty he had displayed in the past, but when urged to "forgive and forget,"

David wisely chose to keep his distance. He knew that words alone weren't any kind of proof that Saul had changed his ways. Sadly, Saul's life ended with no real transformation.

This passage shows that true forgiveness **can** take place without reopening one's life to someone who has only offered words of regret and nothing else. But let me end by saying that there are indeed instances when a person, who previously caused hurt in the lives of others, does surrender to Christ and change for the better. I've seen it happen many times. The key is to look for the *fruit* of change (this is called repentance) and a genuine determination in that person to follow Jesus.

Are Christians required to forgive even when there is no repentance?

I suppose it depends on which passage of Scripture you're looking at. Here's one that supports that idea:

"If your brother sins, rebuke him, and if he repents, forgive him, and if he sins against you seven times in the day, and turns to you seven times, saying, 'I repent,' you must forgive him." (Luke 17:3-4)

But to be fair, there are other passages which speak of extending forgiveness while mentioning nothing of repentance. Check out the two passages below:

Then Peter came up and said to him, "Lord, how often will my brother sin against me, and I forgive him? As many as seven times?" Jesus said to him, "I do not say to you seven times, but

42 PASTOR, I HAVE A QUESTION

seventy-seven times." (Matthew 18:21–22)

Be kind to one another, tenderhearted, forgiving one another, as God in Christ forgave you. (Ephesians 4:32)

When it comes to forgiveness, I have a question of my own: Why would you not want to forgive? As believers we come to learn that unforgiveness is similar to a poison that courses through our hearts, corrupts our thoughts, and ultimately leads to bitterness – and bitterness ruins everything including our relationship with God (see Hebrews 12:15). I think it's better to err on the side of seeing forgiveness as a mandate regardless of what the offender does or doesn't do.

But let me be quick to add that *real* forgiveness is a work of the Holy Spirit. That means if you and I are waiting around for the desire to forgive someone who has hurt us, then we're in for a long wait. Forgiving others is first and foremost an act of obedience. Second, it's a smart thing to do. If you're struggling to forgive someone, you need to come to God and confess that as a weakness and ask for His grace to forgive.

Does God forgive without repentance?
This is a common follow-up question, but I have to be honest that I feel uncomfortable comparing the forgiveness we extend to others with the forgiveness that God offers. The sins and offenses we commit against one another are made *by* sinners, *against* sinners. But the sin that is committed against God is a wholly different matter since we are offending One who is perfect in purity and holiness. In other words, it's not comparing apples to apples. The One eternal, almighty God is on a level that is entirely His own when it comes to such things.

What should I do when forgiveness is expressed but not really shown?

Most Christians know that we must extend forgiveness toward others and many of us may even quickly say "I forgive you" when wronged, but the hard reality of walking out that forgiveness is very difficult.

As the one who confessed wrongdoing and sought forgiveness, it behooves you to walk in patience toward your wounded brother or sister and pray for God's healing grace. God is undoubtedly dealing with that person's heart as well, so ask Him to complete His good work and bring glory to Himself through it. Here's a suggested prayer:

Lord, I know that it's easy to say the words 'I forgive you' but it is extremely hard to live and love as if the person who hurt me is truly forgiven. My brother/sister is struggling with this right now, and that person needs your help to work through the hurt and pain. Help me not to take that person's negative attitude toward me personally. Help me to show my love for them whenever You give me the opportunity. As always, Lord, be glorified through our lives in the name of Jesus Your Son.

What if a believer chooses not to forgive?

This question usually comes up after reading Mark 11:26 which seems to tell us that if we don't forgive, the Father won't forgive us either. But is that really what the verse is saying?

First of all, the context of the passage in Mark 11 is prayer and the things that hinder it for us. Jesus cited unforgiveness as something that greatly hinders prayer because it breaks fellowship with God.

I understand that a lot of people read Mark 11:25–26 and immediately interpret it as saying that forgiving others seems to be listed here as a *requirement* for salvation. They hear Jesus saying, "If you don't forgive others, God won't forgive you," and assume that since a person who doesn't forgive others isn't forgiven by God, then they are also not saved.

But that is *not* what Jesus is saying in that passage. The forgiveness that results in eternal life is, and always will be, a matter of *grace through faith* in the finished work of Jesus on the cross. In other words, it's bestowed as a free gift, which Paul says is *not* of works (Ephesians 2:8–9).

What Jesus is talking about in Mark 11 is something unrelated to salvation. He is speaking of God's parental dealings with His children and He's making us aware that an unforgiving spirit in a child of God causes a break in fellowship with the Lord which then creates a hindrance to prayer.

It's true that when we come to Christ all our sins are forgiven — past, present and future. But that's referring to the forgiveness that results in salvation. There are other issues related to forgiveness that do not affect our salvation, but they do affect our relationship with God. In other words, once a child of God is saved and is now trusting in Jesus for forgiveness, sin can no longer threaten their eternal salvation. But sin can and does threaten one's closeness to God. When you and I sin, it still separates us from God relationally. It drives a wedge between us and God and we find it hard to pray and fellowship with the Lord until we come to Him and confess our wrongdoing. Once we do, the relationship is mended and we can carry on in peace.

The sin that once threatened your eternal destiny has been dealt with at the cross. That is a done deal thanks to the death and resurrection of Jesus. But the daily mess ups and mistakes that we make must still be brought to the Lord in repentance so that nothing stands in the way of walking with Him. That's why we were taught to pray, "forgive us our debts, as we also have forgiven our debtors" (Matthew 6:12). The goal here is to make sure nothing gets in the way of our closeness to God.

Believers who choose not to forgive will be miserable. God's Holy Spirit will be working overtime to get their attention so that they will humble themselves and repent of their hard heart. God is fully able to communicate that unforgiveness is an attitude entirely contrary to His will, and I trust that He will bring all the conviction needed to eventually cause them to turn away from their unforgiveness.

Should a Christian refrain from taking anyone to court?

The Bible forbids a believer to take his brother in Christ to court (see 1 Corinthians 6) but there is no specific prohibition in the Word that I know of which would forbid initiating litigation against an unbeliever.

That being said, we are never free from our obligation to reflect the love of Christ, especially to unbelievers. Nor are we at liberty to violate the command to love our enemies (Matthew 5:44). For these reasons, I think it's critical for believers in Christ to prayerfully search their heart before engaging in any kind of legal action. If there is even the slightest hint of greed, unforgiveness, revenge, bitterness, or any attitude that is contrary to the life of Christ in us — I would strongly advise against moving forward with any legal action. In such a case, it would be better to be wronged or cheated than to engage in court proceedings with improper motives that may end up tarnishing your Christian testimony.

Chapter 4

MAKING DECISIONS

- What does it mean to seek the face of God? 48

- What does decision-making look like in the life of a Christian? 48

- How can I tell God's voice from my own? 49

- What does it mean when someone speaks of the "leading of the Lord"? 53

- What do you do when you need to make time-critical decisions but have no leading from the Lord? 55

What does it mean to seek the face of God?

To *seek* God's face is to earnestly desire His presence to know His heart and will. It is a search for a deeper and closer relationship with God Himself.

The wonderful thing about our God is that He delights to reveal Himself to anyone willing to make the effort. Jesus made a promise along these lines, saying, "**Ask, and it will be given to you; seek, and you will find; knock, and it will be opened to you. For everyone who asks receives, and the one who seeks finds, and to the one who knocks it will be opened**" (Matthew 7:7–8). And the author of Hebrews tells us that God "...**rewards those who seek him**" (11:6).

What does decision-making look like in the life of a Christian?

Walking with the Lord is not so much a matter of figuring out when and where you need to ask for guidance. It's really more about having a surrendered heart that desires the Lord's leading even when you don't ask. In the Old Testament the Lord spoke of Caleb as having "**a different spirit and has followed me fully**" (Numbers 14:24). In other words, the posture of Caleb's heart was to simply follow the Lord in all things.

Like Caleb, we ought to be desiring God's will and direction every single day. That desire for God's leading should also be reflected in our prayers. *"Lord, lead me today and guide my life as You think best. I give my day to You and ask that You would open and close doors according to Your perfect wisdom."* Then, as we go through our day, we can walk in the expectation that He is leading and directing us (see Psalm 32:8).

From time to time, we encounter huge, life-changing decisions and some of them may require us to wait for a very specific directive from the Lord before proceeding. We deal with those kinds of decisions by quieting our hearts in God's presence and spending time in His Word.

But even if other decisions seem small and insignificant, I would never want to think of myself as someone who takes matters into my own hands. I believe the Lord always wants His children to approach every decision-making process with a surrendered attitude and a heart inclined to seek His guidance at all times. Then we can step out into our day with an expectation of the Lord's leading.

How can I tell God's voice from my own?

Hearing from God personally is something Christians seek to do whenever they need the Lord's direction regarding something that isn't specifically covered in the Bible. *"Which job should I choose?" "Is this the person God wants me to marry?" "Should we move to that new area?"* Sometimes it's very difficult to distinguish the Lord's voice from our own desires.

Welcome to the world of living by faith! Here are some things to keep in mind:

50   PASTOR, I HAVE A QUESTION

God wants to speak to you on a spiritual level.
One of the reasons hearing from the Lord is so challenging is because it involves tuning our hearts to God's Spirit. That means we shouldn't be expecting to hear an audible voice from heaven. I mean, sure, God can speak audibly if He wants to, but frankly, spiritual communication is so *much* better.

But that's also where the challenge comes in because our ability to hear God spiritually needs to be developed and that takes time.

Jesus told us that "**God is spirit**" (John 4:24) and that means pursuing the ability to hear His voice is a spiritual quest. Before you get discouraged thinking all this is just too hard, let me quickly assure you that every believer in Christ has been given everything they need to hear God's voice. When you came to faith in Christ, He gave you His Holy Spirit. The Apostle Paul reminds us that every child of God has "the mind of Christ" (1 Corinthians 2:16).

So, why then is hearing God's voice so difficult?

Listed below are just some of the many reasons why it's hard for us to hear God's voice:

- The life of the flesh has hijacked our attention.

- The busyness and the noise in our hearts drown out the voice of God.

- We become impatient because God doesn't respond as quickly as we think He should.

- Our faith muscles are flabby and out of shape because we haven't been exercising them properly.

- Our Bibles have stayed closed much too often.

MAKING DECISIONS   51

In light of these common issues, let me share the following tips:

Change your focus.
We know Jesus told us to "**seek first the Kingdom of God**" (Matthew 6:33) but often our attention gets redirected to fleshly pursuits and interests. The Apostle Paul warned us that "**those who live according to the flesh set their minds on the things of the flesh**" (Romans 8:5). I really believe this is where we need to come clean to the Lord and just confess that our focus has been on all the wrong things and we're in need of a spiritual course-correction. You'll find the Lord responding quickly to your request to help "**set your minds on things that are above**" (Colossians 3:2) and, as a result, hearing His voice will come that much easier.

Learn to quiet your heart.
Learning to hear God's voice means learning to quiet all the other voices that are clamoring for your attention — including your own! David said to the Lord, "**I have calmed and quieted my soul**" (Psalm 131:2). Remember, the soul is the seat of our intellect and emotions, and over time it's possible for the soul to become overstimulated to the point that the noise within our hearts and minds grows to a deafening level. Learning to quiet the noise is essential to hearing from God, so when you come for prayer be sure you're taking the time to just sit in His presence and wait on Him. Don't talk, just sit quietly and focus on Him and Him alone. Breathe. Ask Him to quiet your soul.

Develop patience.
Our modern approach to life (e.g., express lanes and fast food drive-throughs) can be counterproductive to hearing from God because they tend to foster an expectation that life ought to move quickly. But I've learned over the years that God is never in a hurry, and if I want to hear His heart on a

52 PASTOR, I HAVE A QUESTION

matter, I'm the one who needs to adjust my expectations to His timeline, not the other way around.

God has promised that He will give us the wisdom and direction we seek (James 1:5) but the real question is, *how long are we willing to wait for the answer?* Learning to be patient in prayer is essential. David gives this perfect exhortation: "**Wait for the LORD; be strong, and let your heart take courage; wait for the LORD**!" (Psalm 27:14). We need that reminder every single day.

Exercise your faith.
Christians forget that it also takes faith to hear from God. But faith is like a muscle — it becomes flabby and weak if you don't use it regularly. Then when a need arises that demands some real faith, we often find ourselves struggling just to stay in the race. Once again, James reminds us that when we ask of God, we are to "**ask in faith, with no doubting**" (James 1:6). God responds to our faith, so if you're weak in that area the chances are good that you will also struggle hearing from God. Thankfully, when we come humbly before God and confess our weaknesses and shortcomings, we know that God understands and is ready to give us whatever we need. Ask God to help you to have a strong faith.

And finally...

Let the Word transform your mind.
In Romans 12:2, the Apostle Paul tells us to "**be transformed by the renewal of your mind, that by testing you may discern what is the will of God**."

Knowing God's will comes so much easier when our hearts and minds are being transformed by God. This happens as we continue to expose ourselves to the wisdom and insight found only in God's powerful Word. We can then take that knowledge and insight and use them to "test" situations to determine whether they are from God or not.

Remember, knowing the Word is the same as learning to know the heart of God. Once you know God's heart, you find yourself more able to discern the things that please Him as well the things that grieve Him.

What does it mean when someone speaks of the "leading of the Lord"?

It's very difficult to know what people may mean when they use the phrase "leading of the Lord" but I think they are generally speaking of how the Holy Spirit is leading them toward a particular decision or response. And this is something God promises He will do for us, as seen in several passages such as the following:

I will instruct you and teach you in the way you should go; I will counsel you with my eye upon you. (Psalm 32:8)

As to *how* the Holy Spirit leads, that can differ from person to person. God doesn't lead us all the same way and it's impossible to nail down one universal method of detecting God's leading.

For some people the leading of the Lord comes through Scripture. They pray and ask God to direct their steps and then in the course of their Bible reading, they come to a place where they feel the Lord is speaking through the Scriptures to bring specific direction. Others depend on hearing something as the Word is being taught. Over the years I have had

54   PASTOR, I HAVE A QUESTION

many people approach me after teaching and tell me that something in the ministry of the Word spoke what they felt was a specific direction from the Lord for their lives.

Still others look for what the Bible calls the "still small voice" (see 1 Kings 19:12) of God during their prayer time or when they're quieting their heart before the Lord and inclining their ears to hear His voice. (I want to be careful to add that although many Christians believe this method is more spiritual than the others, I don't believe that to be the case.)

Listening for God's leading can be very challenging because we're usually emotionally invested in whatever decisions we're facing. This makes listening difficult, especially if the Lord is telling us something we don't want to hear.

You need to discover the way the Lord wants to speak to you. But don't forget that there are no shortcuts to prayer and waiting on the Lord. We must also remember that God challenges all of us not to lean on our own understanding (Proverbs 3:5). That means being careful not to do what you think is best but to wait for God's wisdom.

When you're waiting on God, it's often very helpful to employ some form of fasting and seek the prayerful intercession of others so that you might be given "ears to hear."

What do you do when you need to make time-critical decisions but have no leading from the Lord?

I've always felt that decisions with a deadline attached to them are among the most challenging and, quite honestly, the most dangerous to bring before the Lord. That's because asking God to respond before a particular deadline has never seemed like a wise move and you're almost guaranteed to get frustrated. When that happens, I find that Christians usually stop praying and just do whatever they think is best.

The fact is, there are times when life presents us with deadlines and there's nothing we can do about them. A prospective employer needs an answer within a week, or you need to decide whether to undergo elective surgery and have two weeks to make up your mind. What do you do when life doesn't give you enough time to really pray and hear from God — or you pray and don't hear anything?

When a deadline is forcing you to make a decision, all you can really do is ask God to guide your decision and then take a step of faith. Sometimes there just isn't time, but God understands. If you bring your concern to Him and pray for His grace to cover whatever choice is made, you can be sure He won't withdraw His providential guidance just because you had a deadline. Trust that the Lord is bigger than your time constraints.

But let me address the larger issue of determining the best way to hear God's voice when you're seeking His direction. You might be interested to know that God's people have been struggling with this sort of thing for a very long time. You are certainly not alone and you definitely shouldn't feel rejected by God.

56 PASTOR, I HAVE A QUESTION

There are three ways believers can seek to know God's direction:

1. Hearing directly from His Holy Spirit

2. Hearing through the Scriptures

3. Hearing God's voice through the counsel of trustworthy believers

Let me explain each of these in a bit more detail:

Hearing directly from the Holy Spirit
Hearing from God directly is the most popular means by which people expect to hear from the Lord but it's also one of the most challenging. Getting quiet enough to hear God's voice is increasingly difficult in our busy, jam-packed world. God communicates through His Spirit to our spirit, and that takes real practice on our part to be a good listener. This is where fasting comes into play. You need to remove every distraction and tune into God's voice.

Hearing through the Scriptures
Don't underestimate determining God's direction through the Word. I have known believers who would sit down and begin reading through the Scriptures, determined not to stop until they receive an answer from the Lord. You'd be surprised how powerful and effective it can be to seek the Lord's heart through the ministry of the Word.

Hearing through the counsel of trustworthy believers
One thing Christians often forget is that we were never meant to live our Christian lives solo. We are part of a family and we ought to take advantage of it. That means being able to find mature and trustworthy believers and getting their counsel. God can certainly use such people to speak into our lives. But beware, I am *not* suggesting you get other people

to hear God for you. I'm talking about getting godly counsel that will help you zero in on God's direction for your life by applying God's Word to your situation. Remember, the people you choose as counselors need to have a proven track record of their own and you should be seeing the fruit of the Spirit in their lives.

Let me also share a word about patience. We've lost something special in our modern, fast-paced society and that is the blessing of going slow. We've adjusted our hearts to the breakneck pace of a constant urgency of events and we demand that God meet us in the midst of that pace. Don't be shocked if He doesn't oblige. The eternal God has his own timetable, and we would be wise to conform to His pace rather than insisting He adjust to ours.

The *Autobiography of George Muller* is a wonderful book to read for anyone wanting to know more about prayer and hearing from God. George Muller was a man of incredible patience while waiting for the Lord. He kept a prayer journal of all his petitions, and it wasn't uncommon for him to literally pray for months and even years before getting an answer from the Lord. But that never discouraged him. George rarely concerned himself with trying to influence God's timing — he just kept asking.

Let me say one more thing concerning this matter of hearing from God. Every believer must take seriously the Scripture passages that speak of removing barriers between us and our risen Lord. What barriers, you ask? I'm talking about the barriers created by sin.

In Isaiah we're told:

Behold, the LORD's hand is not shortened, that it cannot save, or his ear dull, that it cannot hear; but your iniquities have

58   PASTOR, I HAVE A QUESTION

made a separation between you and your God, and your sins have hidden his face from you so that he does not hear. (Isaiah 59:1–2)

Marital strife can also hinder our prayers. Peter said:

Likewise, husbands, live with your wives in an understanding way, showing honor to the woman as the weaker vessel, since they are heirs with you of the grace of life, so that your prayers may not be hindered. (1 Peter 3:7)

I'm not saying this is what's going on in your case since I don't have that kind of insight to say for sure. But can you afford to neglect the possibility? Ask the Lord to reveal anything in your life that may have driven a wedge that now prevents you from hearing God.

While you're at it, search your heart for any unforgiveness or ungodly attitude toward others that may be lingering in your heart. This too can greatly hinder your communication with the Lord.

Did you know that Jesus told a parable for the purpose of encouraging us to pray and not give up? You can find it in Luke 18:1–8.

Don't stop pressing in!

Chapter 5

HOW SHOULD WE RESPOND TO...

- How do I respond to people who say that I have "blind faith"? 60

- How should we respond to unbelievers? 61

- Are we always to obey the government – despite corruption and leaders condoning things such as homosexuality and abortion? 62

- How do we love homosexuals without condoning their sin? 64

- Luke 6:30 says we are to "give to everyone who begs." How then should we respond to people panhandling? 67

- How should Christians respond to the Prosperity or Word-Faith Movement? 68

How do I respond to people who say that I have "blind faith"?

To claim that someone has "blind faith" is to suggest that there is absolutely no evidence for what an individual holds as true. In other words, they are telling you there is *nothing* that backs up your beliefs in any way. For anyone to make such a claim about Christians only proves one thing: that person knows nothing about the Bible or Christianity. There may be some belief systems in this world that truly require blind faith, but ours certainly isn't one of them!

If someone ever told me my faith was blind, I'd say, *"Your statement suggests that there is no evidence supporting the things I hold to be true. What specific Christian beliefs do you claim to require blind faith?"*

Then, of course, I would need to be ready for their response. It might include doubts about the reliability of the Bible or perhaps the existence of God, or some other topic. All believers need to be prepared to give an answer for the reason for our hope (see 1 Peter 3:15). But let me just say that you should never consider yourself at a deficit in this discussion. The Christian faith has the most incredible evidence known to man, and the followers of Jesus need to know what that evidence is and how to defend it.

I heartily recommend the book *Know What You Believe* by Paul E. Little, as well as its companion book *Know Why You Believe* by the same author.

How should we respond to unbelievers?

It's incredibly easy to let frustration boil over when we see the blatant rebellion among unbelievers today. But we cannot forget that these are the very individuals that we are called to reach with the Good News. And if we're angry, we will not be able to effectively reach them for Christ. As James wrote, "**the anger of man does not produce the righteousness of God**" (James 1:20).

As much as our anger would like to be satisfied by seeing God rain judgment down on the defiant, we are reminded that "**God did not send his Son into the world to condemn the world, but in order that the world might be saved through him**" (John 3:17). And we, the Body of Christ, are here to continue that ministry until our Lord returns. It is not a ministry of condemnation, but rather one of compassion. We're told that when Jesus saw the crowds coming to Him, He viewed them as "**harassed and helpless, like sheep without a shepherd**" (Matthew 9:36). We must think of unbelievers in that same way.

We also must never forget that we were once in the same place. The Apostle Paul wrote down for the Corinthians a list of those who would not inherit the kingdom of God and then he added these words: "**And that is what some of you were**" (1 Corinthians 6:11 NIV). In the same verse he then gently reminded them *why* they were no longer listed among the lost, saying, "**But you were washed, you were sanctified, you were justified in the name of the Lord Jesus Christ and by the Spirit of our God.**"

We cannot afford to forget that we were once objects of God's wrath — cut off and without hope in this world. But Jesus saved us by His incredible mercy, and it's not because of our goodness or value, but simply because of His goodness seen through the death of Jesus on our behalf.

Showing love to those who would see themselves as our enemies is never easy but it is imperative. That's why we must rely completely on the power and presence of God's Holy Spirit to do just that. The starting point is setting aside our anger and surrendering ourselves as instruments of His amazing loving kindness. As Jesus said when he gave the Sermon on the Mount, "**Blessed are the peacemakers, for they shall be called sons of God**" (Matthew 5:9).

Are we always to obey the government despite corruption and leaders condoning things such as homosexuality and abortion?

I imagine some of the early believers struggled with the same sort of question back when the Apostle Paul wrote to the Christians in Rome telling them to obey the governing authorities. He said:

Let every person be subject to the governing authorities. For there is no authority except from God, and those that exist have been instituted by God. (Romans 13:1)

They might have wondered if Paul truly understood who he was telling them to obey since the "governing authorities" in Rome were not known for being friendly toward Christians. In fact, those same governing authorities eventually sentenced Paul to death and, according to Church tradition, did the same to most of the original Apostles. How could Paul ask the believers to respect and obey that kind of leadership?

When Paul wrote that we should obey the governing authorities, he was aware of the corruption that had taken place in the hearts of men due to sin. He knew full well that some of the worst of those men had risen and would continue to rise to power in the government. So, what does Romans 13:1 really say? Here are some key insights we get from the verse:

1. Respecting authority is respecting God. Paul clearly states in the passage above that "there is no authority except from God, and those that exist have been instituted by God." In other words, God is behind the authority of man. When we obey the laws of the land, we show respect for the governing authorities. And when we respect the governing authorities, we are respecting and obeying God as well.

2. Respecting does not mean agreeing. Like you, I have some grave differences in philosophy with the current administration. But if I were ever given the opportunity to speak face to face with our president, I would certainly be respectful toward him and maintain an attitude that honored him as a human being and as my president. But I would also speak my mind and express to the best of my ability where I felt his administration and our nation has gone wrong. It is possible for people to express their differences while maintaining an attitude of mutual respect and civility.

3. Respect doesn't necessarily mean obedience. Governments established by men are not the final voice of authority for believers. The only absolute authority in our lives is God, and no human can usurp that position. When the Jewish ruling council attempted to do just that — demanding that the disciples stop preaching in the name of Jesus — Peter and John respectfully replied, "Whether it is right in the sight of God to listen to you rather than to God, you must judge, for we cannot but speak of what we have seen and heard" (Acts 4:19–20). They respectfully declined to acquiesce to the threats leveled against them and made it clear they would continue telling people about Jesus, citing the fact that God's authority trumped that of any human court.

This is called "civil disobedience," but Christians ought never to enter into such a thing lightly. We are to always be respectful and honoring to those who have positions of authority over us. It is only when obeying the governing authorities would require us to violate a clear directive from the Lord that we have the freedom to respectfully decline. In that case we must be obedient to the authority that is higher than any government created by man. Jesus is our final authority, and the most powerful government official must ultimately bow the knee before the King of kings.

How do we love homosexuals without condoning their sin?

Ultimately, our position on homosexuality ought to be firmly centered around the unchanging Word of God. However, there are many believers who respond by saying, "It's not our place to judge." But are they correct?

Do Not Judge
It is true that the Bible says we are not to judge, but if you read the entire passage (something very few people take the time to do), you quickly discover that Jesus was talking about making hypocritical judgments. In other words, judging someone for something when you're guilty of the same thing! It's found in Matthew 7:1 and verses following.

HOW SHOULD WE RESPOND TO... 65

Many Christians *naively* believe that we are never to judge anyone or anything. That's just not true. Later on in the very same chapter of Matthew, Jesus spoke of making judgments by testing the fruit of certain individuals to make sure they were genuine. And later in John's Gospel account, Jesus is actually quoted as saying, "**Do not judge by mere appearances, but judge with right judgment**" (John 7:24). In the Gospel of Luke He said, "**Why do you not judge for yourselves what is right?**" (Luke 12:57). It seems that when people are yelling "Judge not!" they somehow miss those passages.

You simply can't go through life without making judgments. It's not possible. Every day we make judgements on several matters, whether big or small, to make good decisions. If a mother, struggling to contain her toddler in public, was approached by a very suspicious-looking stranger offering to help her, would you tell her that it's wrong to make a judgment about the stranger and that she should just hand her child over? Of course not! Since she's responsible for the safety of her child, she is required to make many judgments throughout a single day.

Let's be clear about something: If you and I communicate to others that we have made an assessment about homosexuality based on God's Word, we're not going to be showered with praise. In fact, people will use the opportunity to mock and ridicule our beliefs. There's nothing we can do about that — it's just the way things are. But what we can do is have the right attitude.

Speaking the Truth in Love
Just because we assess things to be wrong or contrary to the Word of God doesn't mean we are free to condemn the people who do such things. The Lord Jesus Himself said that "**God did not send his Son into the world to condemn the world, but to save the world through him**" (John 3:17 NIV). If

Jesus didn't come to condemn, then neither should we. Our job is rather to point people to the cross.

Christians should be marked by a gentle and tender spirit toward homosexuals and their concerns. Jesus died for them no less than for anyone else, and we need to convey God's intense love in every opportunity we get.

So, is it Wrong to Call Homosexuality Sin?
Our modern cultural climate has created a hostile environment for labeling anything as sinful. I once had someone tell me it was hateful and cruel to say that anything someone did was wrong. (Let me be quick to add that I don't consider it my job to go around telling people they are wrong or sinful, but quite often the subject comes up about what the Bible says or doesn't say.) So, are we wrong to even communicate such things?

The Gospel of John recounts a time when Jesus was confronted with a woman caught in the act of adultery. The people standing around wanted Him to condemn the woman and stone her to death. But Jesus spoke gently to the woman and told her that He did not condemn her. But He didn't stop there. Do you recall what else He said? It was, "**Go now and leave your life of sin**." (John 8:11 NIV).

Our Lord's refusal to condemn the woman should not be seen as a declaration of approval or agreement with her sinful lifestyle. He refused to condemn her, but He also refused to leave her with any kind of confusion concerning the act in which she had been involved. That's the kind of balance we need when dealing with the subject of homosexuality.

Luke 6:30 says we are to "give to everyone who begs." How then should we respond to people panhandling?

The New American Standard Bible (NASB) renders Luke 6:30 this way:

Give to everyone who asks of you, and whoever takes away what is yours, do not demand it back.

The point of this passage is that believers are to be characterized by generosity and compassion, showing mercy and kindness even if the person doesn't deserve those things. Why? Because we are the recipients of God's mercy when we least deserved it.

So, how should we interpret Luke 6:30? Here's a quote from the Tyndale Bible Commentary that expresses a wonderful balance of thought on this matter:

If Christians took this one absolutely literally there would soon be a class of saintly paupers, owning nothing, and another of prosperous idlers and thieves. It is not this that Jesus is seeking, but a readiness among his followers to give and give and give. Love must be ready to be deprived of everything if need be. Of course, in a given case it may not be the way of love to give. But it is love that must decide whether we give or withhold, not a regard for our possessions... *

Isn't that good? Love is to be our motive — loving people more than our possessions. But when is giving *not* an act of love?

I don't think there's any substitute for Spirit-led giving. If the willingness to give is present and the believer is listening to the Father's voice, giving will be generous and helpful. But indiscriminately handing out cash to someone who will only take it and buy liquor or drugs is *not* being benevolent or helpful.

*Leon Morris, "Luke: An Introduction and Commentary," *Tyndale New Testament Commentaries*, Inter-Varsity Press. 1988.

How should Christians respond to the Prosperity or Word-Faith Movement?

I believe the "prosperity" or "word-faith" teaching is full of imbalance and such things almost always create danger. For starters, this teaching focuses the heart of the believer almost exclusively on material blessings and places the weight of seeing such things come to pass entirely on the faith of the recipient. It is then quick to accuse believers of having insufficient faith when prayers for healing or blessing aren't immediately answered.

One of the fundamental errors of this movement is the belief that physical healing is guaranteed as part of the work that Jesus accomplished for us on the cross. They often quote Isaiah 53:5 that says, "...**with His wounds we are healed**," claiming that in the sacrifice of Jesus we have been given physical health and healing. This is a *very* superficial conclusion based on the appearance of the word "healed" which is assumed to refer to physical healing. However, the context of that passage, as well as the passage in which it is quoted

HOW SHOULD WE RESPOND TO... 69

from in the New Testament (1 Peter 2:24), is **spiritual healing**.

The word-faith movement treats God as if He were a mindless vending machine. If we simply deposit the required number of coins (faith) and push the right button, we are guaranteed to receive whatever we want. It is true that God looks at our faith, but He is not obligated by it. Our faith does not overrule the sovereignty of the God who always knows what is best for His children.

I am not saying that God does not heal. He *does* and I have seen it. At our fellowship we continue to pray for people to be healed and we anoint them with oil according to the Word of God. However, the belief that physical healing is a *guarantee to all believers* and that God *always heals* in every instance where faith is applied is simply and biblically untrue.

If your church is fixated on a prosperity message, you may need to find a new community of believers with whom to fellowship. I find that most prosperity-based churches do *not* teach through the Bible from Genesis to Revelation, but instead camp on specific passages that support their views. In such an environment, true and healthy spiritual maturity may be hard to come by.

❖

Chapter 6

THE CHRISTIAN LIFE

- How can I overcome anxiety? 72

- What should I do if I don't feel forgiven by God? 74

- What does it mean to fear the Lord? 76

- What does it mean to love God with all your heart, soul, mind, and strength? 77

- What is worship? 79

- What should I do when my heart has grown cold toward God? 81

- How can I find the area where God wants me to serve? 82

- Does God command us to tithe? 84

- How do we store up treasures in heaven? 85

- Why is participating in a church body important? 86

- How do I meditate on God's Word? 90

THE CHRISTIAN LIFE 71

- How should Christians view their own past? 91

- Isaiah 53:3 tells us that "by His wounds we are healed." From what are we healed? 95

- How can we take comfort in the Lord rather than the things of this world? 96

- Is hypnotism a safe practice for believers? 97

72   PASTOR, I HAVE A QUESTION

How can I overcome anxiety?

Anxiety is a terrible thing. It makes us feel vulnerable and defenseless. It kicks in when we focus exclusively on our problems or challenges and because our faith is weak, we give in to fear and become overwhelmed by it. The key to overcoming anxiety is to bring our thoughts and concerns under control and to build up our faith.

Engaging Self-control

Controlling thoughts is challenging, especially when we have a history of allowing our darker thoughts to run free. But the good news is that God has given us the fruits of His Holy Spirit, one of which is self-control (Galatians 5:23).

The thing we need to realize about the fruits of the Holy Spirit is that they don't just magically or automatically become active. There is a need on our part to allow these characteristics of God's Spirit to have a greater place of freedom to operate in our lives. It means that through prayer and meditation on the Word we have to invite the Spirit to help us master our thoughts and ponderings.

But we do this not just by controlling negative thoughts. We must also fill our heart with thoughts that are uplifting and edifying. Remember the promise given to us in Isaiah 26:3.

You keep him in perfect peace whose mind is stayed on you, because he trusts in you.

Notice the condition for this perfect peace: a mind stayed on God. In the New Living Translation, a person whose mind is "stayed" on God is described as one "whose thoughts are fixed" on the Lord.

So what kinds of thoughts should an anxious person be

THE CHRISTIAN LIFE 73

thinking about? The Apostle Paul has a suggestion:

Finally, brothers, whatever is true, whatever is honorable, whatever is just, whatever is pure, whatever is lovely, whatever is commendable, if there is any excellence, if there is anything worthy of praise, think about these things. (Philippians 4:8)

Your Own Worst Enemy

I said earlier that anxiety is, in part, the result of a diminished faith in God. But that doesn't mean worriers have no faith. They do! It's just misplaced.

I find that those who struggle with anxious thoughts actually have a *lot* of faith — just in themselves. They trust their own fearful thoughts *more* than they trust the Word of God. In other words, they choose to trust their anxious thoughts above and beyond the character of God. And that is precisely why God gave us this well-known passage in His Word:

Trust in the Lord with all your heart, and do not lean on your own understanding. In all your ways acknowledge him, and he will make straight your paths. (Proverbs 3:5–6)

The exhortation here is to reject the thoughts that originate from self and trust the Lord instead. It requires a conscious effort to say to oneself, *"My thoughts cannot be trusted. My fears are not reliable. My heart is deceitful and always thinks the worst. I choose to focus my thoughts on God's Word and believe His promises instead."*

Don't Forget Repentance

There's one more element of breaking free from anxiety which must not be neglected and that is *repentance.* People who struggle with anxiety are usually so familiar with this aspect of their lives that they don't see it as *sin.* But fearful and anxious thoughts are the opposite of faith, and when we give in to fear we are missing the mark.

I don't say that to generate feelings of guilt, but rather to highlight the fact that God has provided a means for us to deal with our sin and find His wonderful forgiveness. This comes when we bring our fears to the cross of Christ and confess them for what they truly are — sin. When fearful and anxious thoughts surface, bring them quickly to Jesus and confess them as wrong and contrary to His will.

Remember this glorious promise from God's Word:

If we confess our sins, he is faithful and just to forgive us our sins and to cleanse us from all unrighteousness. (1 John 1:9)

Before you battle your inner fears, make sure you've brought those sins before the cross and have found God's faithful forgiveness. You will be in a much better place to get on the road to restoring the peace in your heart.

What should I do if I don't feel forgiven by God?

Let's face it, we're all intimately connected to our feelings since they're hardwired in humankind. But the emphasis we've been putting on our feelings has escalated to a point where they have become our go-to lenses through which we view and evaluate our reality. The frightening part for believers is that feelings now take precedence over faith.

If someone *feels* saved, they will experience a satisfaction

THE CHRISTIAN LIFE   75

with that sensation and try their utmost to hang on to it. But if they encounter feelings that suggest they are *not* saved, they are just as likely to be plunged into despair.

The same barometer is used for prayer. I've had people come up to me and say things like: *"Pastor Paul, I don't feel like God is hearing my prayers,"* or *"I'm feeling unfulfilled in my marriage. What should I do?"*

In each of these instances, feelings are exalted as the single most important means of measuring truth and reality. My marriage is gauged by how "in love" I feel with my spouse. My ministry is defined by how fulfilled I feel, and my relationship with God is determined by how accepted and loved I feel.

As a pastor, my job is to continually point believers back to the authority of the Word, and that is exactly what I do. If I am talking with someone who feels unforgiven, I tell that person to read 1 John 1:9 which contains a wonderful promise of forgiveness to those who confess their sins. We read the passage together and I highlight key words to make the text more understandable. But after finishing my exhortation based on that Scripture, they look at me and say in a pained voice, *"Yeah, I see that...but I still don't **feel** forgiven."*

What I've just witnessed is a believer exalting feelings over and above the authority of God's Word. That person knows what the Word says, and yet still chooses to believe that feelings are the final, authoritative guide to judging what is real and what is not.

It's hard for me to overstate the danger this kind of thinking invites. To elevate the heart of man as the means of determining what is true or false is the height of foolishness. Believers forget that their own hearts have been revealed in Scripture as unreliable – purposely deceitful and entirely beyond understanding.

The heart is deceitful above all things, and desperately sick; who can understand it? (Jeremiah 17:9)

In light of this passage from Jeremiah, believers need to repent of this modern form of idolatry and return to the only One who can truly be the guide of all truth, and that is God Himself. The challenge will be turning a deaf ear to their feelings — the voice that once guided their every thought and decision — and returning to the Lord who created them and knows what is best, even when feelings tell them otherwise.

What does it mean to fear the Lord?

I get this question quite often because a modern reader sees the word *fear* and wonders if it means "to be terrified." But that interpretation misses the emphasis of what God is trying to convey when His Word tells us to "fear God."

At its essence, fearing God means to acknowledge and honor the Lord for who He is and to obey His Word. This is what's included in the exhortation to "**fear the LORD, and turn away from evil**" (Proverbs 3:7).

We have all seen practical examples of this in everyday life while driving on the freeway. People are moving along at a brisk pace until someone spots a police car parked alongside the highway with his radar gun pointed at oncoming traffic. Instantly, brake lights beam one after the other as people slow down to avoid being stopped for speeding. Although it may seem somewhat simple, this response to the police officer by those on the freeway is a good example of what it means to fear God. The drivers slow down because they recognize and respect the officer's authority and ability to hold them accountable for their unlawful actions.

When we acknowledge that God is sovereign and all-powerful and that He has this same authority and ability to hold us accountable for our actions, we respond to Him with what the Bible calls a *reverent fear* and we adjust our behavior in keeping with His will, whether revealed in His Word or merely confirmed by our conscience.

What does it mean to love God with all your heart, soul, mind, and strength?

Deuteronomy 6:4–5 says, "**Hear, O Israel: The LORD our God, the LORD is one. You shall love the LORD your God with all your heart and with all your soul and with all your might.**" This is called the *Shema*, and orthodox Jews consider reciting it morning and evening to be among their most sacred duties. When Jesus was asked which of the commandments was the greatest, this is the one He quoted, quickly adding that the command to "love your neighbor as yourself" was no less great (Matthew 22:37–39).

The references to heart, soul, and might (strength) are meant to convey the idea of the whole person. The Lord is therefore commanding that we love God with everything in us.

Having said that, we need to quickly acknowledge that this command can never be fully obeyed by sinful human beings.

78 PASTOR, I HAVE A QUESTION

To love God every hour of every single day of our entire lives without fail is outside of our ability. That's why Jesus needed to come and die on the cross for our sins. Every day we fall short of this lofty ideal. And yet it ought to remain the goal of our lives.

In 2 Kings 23 we read of a king of Judah who loved the Lord as much as was humanly possible. Of King Josiah it is said:

Before him there was no king like him, who turned to the LORD with all his heart and with all his soul and with all his might, according to all the Law of Moses, nor did any like him arise after him. (v. 25)

When you read about the life of King Josiah, you will see all the things he did and how his love for the Lord motivated him to live a life devoted to God. Of course, the way you express your love for God is going to be different, but one thing will be the same: your love for God will consume you.

To love God with all your heart, soul, mind, and strength is to live for God above everything else. It is to use all that God has given you — your heart, your thoughts, and even your physical energy — for Him and His purposes.

Come to think of it, this command is the opposite of how most of us live our lives because, if we're going to be honest, we all spend most of our time living for ourselves. Our goals and efforts are all directed at being happy and feeling fulfilled. But that is a self-centered existence. God wants us to live our lives for Him — to please Him and serve Him. To do that with *nothing* standing in the way is to love the Lord with all your heart, soul, mind, and strength.

What is worship?

It's important to understand the difference between the act of worshiping God and the ways we express our worship. Most people focus on the expressions and neglect the heart, so let's talk about the heart of worship first.

What is worship? Well, the first thing we learn from the Bible is that worship is a spiritual act.

God is spirit, and those who worship him must worship in spirit and truth. (John 4:24)

Jesus spoke the words quoted above and He said that we must worship God "in spirit." But what exactly does that mean? The Apostle Paul gives us insight in his letter to the Romans:

Therefore, I urge you, brothers, in view of God's mercy, to offer your bodies as living sacrifices, holy and pleasing to God--this is your spiritual act of worship. (Romans 12:1 NIV84)

Here, Paul says that our "spiritual act of worship" is presenting our very lives as living sacrifices to the Lord. This means coming to God and surrendering our lives to Him — to live for Him and to serve Him with all our hearts. Under the Old Covenant the people of God would sacrifice animals for various reasons, one of which was to show the worshipper's complete devotion to God. Under the New Covenant we don't sacrifice animals, instead we sacrifice ourselves.

So, according to the Bible, to worship God spiritually means to offer yourself daily to the Lord for His purpose. This is the true essence of worship.

Now, let's talk about the various expressions of worship. The

80 PASTOR, I HAVE A QUESTION

things listed below are some of the ways we express our worship, but they are *not*, in and of themselves, worship:

- singing
- lifting hands
- kneeling
- shouting to the Lord in praise
- dancing

These are all acceptable expressions, but they alone do not qualify as acts of worship. Worship comes from the heart, not from the hands or mouth or feet. Anyone can do any of the things listed above and still *not* worship God.

Think of it this way: Imagine you asked me to define "love" between a husband and wife, and I responded by saying, "Love is kissing and embracing." But wait, people can do those things without being in love. Kissing and embracing can be expressions of love, but they are not what love is. Love is a matter of the heart and therefore springs from the heart and not from the outward actions of the body.

Let's review: Worship is the act of offering oneself to God in surrender to His Lordship.

We can express our worship in many ways, but we must never allow those expressions to be thought of as worship. Worship comes from the heart.

What should I do when my heart has grown cold toward God?

You can't "fix" it, but you can move toward rectifying the situation in a way that allows God to restore your heart toward Him. Here are some steps you can take:

Tell God. Too many believers, when they realize that the state of their heart is not what it should be, skip over this crucial first step — bringing the matter before the Lord. Come to the Lord and simply confess your heart's condition. Tell Him you are aware that your heart needs to be renewed toward Him and ask Him to fill you with a fresh desire to know and draw near to Him.

Ask God to search your heart. King David prayed: "**Search me, O God, and know my heart! Try me and know my thoughts! And see if there be any grievous way in me, and lead me in the way everlasting!**" (Psalm 139:23–24)

Coldness toward God can sometimes be the result of an unknown area of sin, which makes the wisdom of following David's example in prayer even more important. Ask the Lord to search and test your heart to see if there is anything that needs to change. If He shows you something, be quick to obey, remembering the words of Hebrews 3:12–13.

Be consistent with your time in the Word. You simply cannot underestimate the power of daily immersing your heart in God's Word. There is a softening work that takes place when we consistently expose our hearts to the wisdom and beauty of the living Word of God.

Scrutinize your areas of influence. The human heart is like a garden and every day we plant things in it that will affect our relationship with God. Some are helpful and others are not. Movies, music, books, websites, friends, and even our own personal thoughts should all be examined to determine if they are helpful in drawing us near to God or doing the opposite.

How can I find the area where God wants me to serve?

All service must begin from the place of surrender where we say to Jesus, "I am Yours Lord, and I give my life to You." Afterwards, there are steps to knowing specifically where the Lord would have you serve.

Ask God
This first step may sound like a no-brainer, but you'd be surprised how many believers skip it. Be sure you've come to the Lord and expressed your desire to serve. Understand that God wants to bring you into the center of His will so you may walk in the confidence that He will lead you, even if you don't happen to see the path right away.

To what are you inclined?
Often, areas of service are found through our natural (or supernatural) inclination toward a particular area. Do you have a burden for teenagers? How about ministering to seniors? Maybe you love organizing or fixing things. Perhaps God has put a love for music in your heart. The things you are drawn toward may be from the Holy Spirit leading you to a place of ministry. Bring those things to God in prayer and ask Him to open doors according to His will.

Be available and be willing
There are those who will quickly offer their service but are rarely available when the time comes for things to be done. Serving the Lord will involve sacrifice in terms of your time and energy. Make sure your heart is willing.

What needs to be done?
Some people fall prey to "analysis paralysis" when it comes to understanding the exact calling God has upon their lives. As a result, they never actually do anything because they're constantly waiting for that special calling. While you're waiting for specifics of the Lord's calling for your life, just get busy. Look around and see what needs to be done and ask how you can help. One pastor I know came to church and saw how everything on a Sunday was prepared and ready. He knew that there were people working behind the scenes to get it that way so he asked an usher how he could help. He was told that if he was willing to come 30 minutes before the service and stay an hour afterward there were plenty of things for him to do. That's how he started serving.

Stepping Out in Faith
Finding your calling may be a matter of being willing to try various avenues of service just to see what the Lord shows you. Not long after my wife and I started walking with the Lord, we were asked to help out in our church's senior high youth group. At first I was a little dubious about getting involved, but she really wanted to, so we gave it a try. Not long after we started, the person leading the group left it in our hands. I was thrust into a teaching position and it was then I discovered the Lord's gifting in my life — teaching the Scriptures.

Does God command us to tithe?

I understand that tithing was part of the Mosaic Law which we're no longer under. I also know that God is pleased with a cheerful giver. But in Genesis we see that Abraham tithed in an act that predates the Law. Jesus also speaks of tithing in Matthew 23:23 as something of importance. So, should we tithe or not?

You're right, tithing does predate the Mosaic Law, but just because someone is seen doing something in an Old Testament narrative, that doesn't mean we are commanded to do it today. More than that, it is important to realize that the New Covenant is not about keeping rules. God wants His children to be Spirit-led, not governed by external regulations. That's why the Apostle Paul wrote: "**Each one must give as he has decided in his heart, not reluctantly or under compulsion**" (2 Corinthians 9:7).

What Paul is describing in 2 Corinthians is precisely the kind of giving you're seeing in Genesis 14. Abraham didn't give a tenth of his possessions to Melchizedek because he had to or because he was under some external compulsion to comply. He gave because he had determined in his heart to be generous. That's the kind of giving we are exhorted to imitate under the New Covenant.

In the Matthew passage that you referenced, Jesus is simply acknowledging the principle of tithing in the Scripture, but His comments are given in the hearing of Jews prior to the establishment of the New Covenant. The Apostle Paul's remarks in 2 Corinthians are God's present-day instructions for the Church on the subject of Spirit-led giving.

How do we store up treasures in heaven?

The phrase "treasure in heaven" comes from a conversation between Jesus and a rather wealthy young man who had approached Him with a question about eternal life.

Jesus said to him, "If you would be perfect, go, sell what you possess and give to the poor, and you will have treasure in heaven; and come, follow me." (Matthew 19:21)

His reaction to our Lord's challenge proved that the young man was more interested in accumulating earthly treasure than storing up treasure in heaven.*

There are other passages in the Bible that speak of storing up treasure in heaven. Like the passage in Matthew cited above, the way to do that is directly connected to how we use our earthly wealth. Note the passage below:

As for the rich in this present age...They are to do good, to be rich in good works, to be generous and ready to share, thus storing up treasure for themselves as a good foundation for the future, so that they may take hold of that which is truly life. (1 Timothy 6:17–19)

In his letter to the church in Philippi, Paul spoke of heavenly treasures when he wrote:

...even when I was in Thessalonica, you sent me aid again and again when I was in need. Not that I am looking for a gift, but I am looking for what may be credited to your account. (Philippians 4:16–17 NIV84)

The "account" that Paul was referring to existed in heaven. In other words, Paul was looking to see that the Philippians' treasure in heaven might be increased by their generosity here on earth.

Although there are other passages which do a good deal more than suggest that our financial generosity will be amply rewarded by the Lord (see Proverbs 19:17), I don't believe giving one's money is the *only* means of storing up treasures in heaven. In fact, any good works on the part of a believer are more assuredly a way we can store up treasures. God has made that kind of thing abundantly possible by providing good works for us to accomplish (see Ephesians 2:10).

The Parable of the Talents (Matthew 25:14–30; Luke 19:11–27) was given to us to underscore two things: (1) God has given us the temporary use of all kinds of gifts, abilities, and resources to invest in His kingdom; and (2) He will one day ask us to account for how faithfully we have used those things on His behalf. This is unquestionably a key to storing up treasure in heaven.

Why is participating in a church body important? What do we say to people who say they don't need a "man-made institution" like the Church?

Quite honestly, I'm not sure you say anything. Too often we find ourselves saying a lot of things that other people — like the person who made that statement — are not ready to hear. But I will address this for anyone who is genuinely pondering this question.

For starters, the Church is not a man-made institution. Jesus

THE CHRISTIAN LIFE   87

is the One who claimed to be the Originator and the Head of the church.

...on this rock I will build my church, and the gates of Hades will not overcome it. (Matthew 16:18 NIV84)

It was Jesus who started, commissioned, and laid down His life for the Church, and now He empowers it by His Spirit to carry out His redemptive purpose. The Apostle Paul speaks of Jesus as the "Head" of the Church.

...speaking the truth in love, we will in all things grow up into him who is the Head, that is, Christ. From him the whole body, joined and held together by every supporting ligament, grows and builds itself up in love, as each part does its work. (Ephesians 4:15–16 NIV84)

A study of the New Testament makes it abundantly clear that the Church is made up of redeemed individuals who have placed their hope in Christ for the salvation of their souls. The Church is *not* a building but a *body* of believers, called by the Name of Christ and commissioned to go forth in His light and truth.

That said, I am aware that there have been instances when the church has been assaulted and, in some cases, commandeered by human control and the corruption of sinful leaders. In fact, studying church history can be a disturbing and discouraging endeavor. But the question every Christian needs to ask is this: *Does that history give me the right to reject the Church and toss it aside?*

I believe when some people speak despairingly of the Church, they are really targeting organized religion which they see as one and the same with the Church but is in fact not the same at all. Organized religion is man's attempt to seize and control that which was designed by God to be led

88   PASTOR, I HAVE A QUESTION

by humble and broken individuals who fear God and seek His direction and will. A human-run institution of committees and programs that too often commandeer the leading of the Holy Spirit is a far cry from God's intended design.

One thing every redeemed child of God needs to remember is that, like it or not, by placing their hope in Christ for salvation, they have been made members of His Church.

Consequently, you are...members of God's household, built on the foundation of the apostles and prophets, with Christ Jesus himself as the chief cornerstone. (Ephesians 2:19–20 NIV84)

Rather than criticizing the Church for its obvious imperfections and opting out of any participation, it ought to be the responsibility of every child of God to prayerfully seek out a place of worship that is in keeping with God's design for the Church as revealed in the Scriptures.

Here are some of the things you should look for:

1. A Solidly Biblical Statement of Faith. When you attend a church, ask them for a written copy of what they believe. When you get it, compare it to the Word of God to make sure it matches up.

2. Biblical Leadership. Ask questions about how the leadership of the fellowship is set up. God gives us a lot of leeway in the New Testament for establishing and running a local fellowship, but here are some important things you should look for:

- The pastor shouldn't be a "hireling" whose position is based on the whims of popular vote. Neither should he be a dictator with limitless authority.

- Leadership should exemplify the fruits of the Holy

THE CHRISTIAN LIFE 89

Spirit (Galatians 5:22–23). Know what those fruits are and expect to see them displayed in church leaders.

- The pastor should be able to teach God's Word in an understandable and clear manner that leaves you feeling well-fed and challenged.

- There shouldn't be an undue emphasis on money and the leaders should not be participants in financial extravagance.

3. A Heart for the Community. A church fellowship should be actively reaching out to the local community and beyond by sharing the Gospel.

4. Signs of Growth. Is there a balanced mix of younger and older members, with new people coming?

5. Biblical and Balanced Worship. Too many churches engage in unbiblical and unhealthy expressions of worship that only serve to make people feel uncomfortable. The Apostle Paul wrote that everything should be done "decently and in order" (1 Corinthians 14:40). The fellowship you attend should follow this biblical pattern. I'm not saying it should be boring, but it's important that it's orderly.

6. God's Word as the Final Authority. A balanced fellowship shouldn't emphasize emotional responses and personal experience over God's Word. Emotions and experiences are fine, but God's Word should always have the final say.

7. Healthy and Stable Fellowship. The church community should see itself as part of the larger network of the Body of Christ. Avoid a fellowship that leaves you with the impression that they have something that other churches don't have.

There is no such thing as a perfect fellowship. That's because the members are people just like you and me — possessing sinful hearts. But just because churches are fraught with problems doesn't mean any of us has the right to forsake a place of worship with other believers. God wants you to be connected to a place that's healthy and growing in His grace. So, go do your homework and spend time in God's Word as you seek His guidance on this matter.

How do I meditate on God's Word?

The Bible doesn't give instructions on meditating on the Word. In fact, the word **meditate** (which means "to think deeply or focus one's mind for a period of time") doesn't even appear in the New Testament. That said, mediating on God's Word is a good practice. Here are what I hope will be helpful suggestions:

1. Take a verse or passage and read it several times.

2. Pray for the Lord's illuminating work in your heart.

3. Write the passage out on a piece of paper and highlight or encircle what you believe to be the key words.

4. Think about or look up the definitions of those key words even if you're familiar with them.

5. Ask yourself some of the following questions:

- Does this chapter/passage/verse teach or reveal anything about God?

- Is there an example or instruction about godliness in this passage?

- Is there an example or instruction about sin that I need to take note of? (Is there a command to obey?)

- Is there a promise for me to take hold of?

- What can I praise and thank the Lord for based on this passage?

- What would the Lord have me **do** or what areas of my life do I need to surrender to the Lordship of Jesus? (Commit this to prayer.)

Doing these things will help you as you meditate on God's Word.

How should Christians view their own past?

It's true that the past can serve as a learning ground that can deepen our understanding and shape our character; but if we're not cautious, it can also be a miry pit, trapping and keeping us from recognizing and enjoying the blessings of God.

The Past is a Teacher
There are times in God's Word when the Lord counsels His people to consider the events of the past so that the lessons of the past might shed light on their current situation.

Review the past for me, let us argue the matter together;

92 PASTOR, I HAVE A QUESTION

state the case for your innocence. Your first father sinned; your spokesmen rebelled against me. (Isaiah 43:26–27 NIV84)

In this passage the Lord is calling His people to draw insight from the events of the past by reminding them of mankind's original sin through Adam. In other words, God is helping them recognize how sin has separated them from Him.

Dwelling on the Past
While there is a place and time to recollect the events of the past to gain a heart of wisdom, there is also a time to just release and let go. Once more in Isaiah, we see the Lord saying something else about dealing with the past. Here He says:

"Forget the former things; do not dwell on the past. See, I am doing a new thing! Now it springs up; do you not perceive it? I am making a way in the desert and streams in the wasteland." (Isaiah 43:18–19 NIV84)

Here is an important word from the Lord on the dangers of focusing too much on the past. After a strong exhortation to forget the former things, the Lord says, "**See, I am doing a new thing! Do you not perceive it?**" This question is vital to understanding how dwelling on the past affects us. The fact is, when we are mired in the thoughts and events of the past and wallowing in the hurts and pain of yesterday, we become oblivious to the "new" things the Lord is doing all around us. That's why God asks, "Do you not perceive it?" The perspective of a person who struggles with letting go of the past gets blurry and becomes a hindrance to "seeing" the good things the Lord is doing all around their life.

Only God can make a way where there seems to be no way. But we must get our eyes off the past and look upon the power of the Lord. The writer of Hebrews tells us to "fix our eyes on Jesus, the author and perfecter of our faith" (12:2 NIV84). This cannot be done when our eyes are fixed on our past.

Letting Go of Hurts
Modern psychology suggests that the way to be healed of our past is to go back and "relive" those events. God, on the other hand, tells us to learn from them and let them go! The problem is, sometimes our past is full of painful memories which can be very hard, if not impossible, to forget. Those who are unable to move on from the past usually can't come to a place of forgiving those who had hurt them before.

The good news is that God doesn't expect us to conquer our past all by ourselves. Our loving Heavenly Father is the One who longs to take our past and bring healing and wholeness to the wounds we've received. The question is whether or not we are willing to let go and forgive. Notice in the following passage how the Apostle Paul refers to his Lord:

Praise be to the God and Father of our Lord Jesus Christ, the Father of compassion and the God of all comfort, who comforts us in all our troubles, so that we can comfort those in any trouble with the comfort we ourselves have received from God. (2 Corinthians 1:3–4 NIV84)

Paul called God "the Father of compassion and the God of all comfort," but how many Christians today truly know God in this way? How many have openly come to the Lord and allowed Him to bring His perfect comfort into the wounded and darkened areas of their hearts? I believe the number is quite low, and so we see the Body of Christ running after other methods of bringing healing to their tortured souls. What a tragedy! If we would only release, forgive, and move on.

94 PASTOR, I HAVE A QUESTION

One woman who was all too familiar with tragedy and unforgiveness was Corrie ten Boom. Born in April 1892 in Amsterdam, Netherlands, Corrie lived during WWII and personally experienced the horror of the Nazi invasion of her homeland. Corrie, her sister Betsie, and their elderly father were all arrested by the Nazis and charged with hiding Jews. Corrie and Betsie were taken to a German concentration camp where they were exposed to the most horrific conditions imaginable. Betsie finally died in that hellish concentration camp, but through a cleric's error, Corrie was released.

After the war, Corrie opened their home to minister to the people who had been so shamefully and tragically treated by the Nazis. She observed one common element in those who were able to heal from the events of those horrible years. She wrote:

*Those who were able to forgive their former enemies were able also to return to the outside world and rebuild their lives, no matter what the physical scars. Those who nursed their bitterness remained invalids. It was as simple and as horrible as that.**

May the Lord give you the strength today to give Him your past.

*Corrie ten Boom with Jamie Buckingham, "Tramp for the Lord," (Pennsylvania: CLC Publications, 2011), 57.

Isaiah 53:3 tells us that "by His wounds we are healed." From what are we healed?

The Apostle Peter not only quoted this passage from the Old Testament, but he also explained what it means. It goes like this:

He himself bore our sins in his body on the tree, that we might die to sin and live to righteousness. By his wounds you have been healed. For you were straying like sheep, but have now returned to the Shepherd and Overseer of your souls. (1 Peter 2:24–25)

Peter explains that the "healing" Isaiah prophesied about was a spiritual healing that allowed those of us who were "straying like sheep" to return to God. This healing was made possible by Jesus who paid the penalty for our sins and removed the barrier that separated us from God.

Many in the Body of Christ have assumed that the healing mentioned in that verse refers to the healing of our physical bodies. That belief has spawned an entire movement predicated upon the idea that the guarantee of physical healing is included within the work of redemption that Jesus accomplished for us on the cross.

As much as I would like to believe it, I simply cannot subscribe to the idea that physical healing is guaranteed to us based on the sufferings of Jesus Christ on the cross. The Bible simply does not support that idea.

How can we take comfort in the Lord rather than the things of this world?

I must confess I really like the things in this life that bring me comfort. The opposite is also true: I usually try to avoid anything that makes me uncomfortable. I don't think I'm alone in this. In fact, when I look around, I see an incredible number of things that people are running after to bring a modicum of comfort into their lives. Some of them aren't bad in and of themselves. In fact, some are *needs* that God created us to have.

I can't blame anyone for seeking comfort. Living in this fallen and sin-corrupted world brings plenty of discomfort into our days, and I suppose it's quite natural for us to want to pull the covers up to our chin and stay warm and cozy for as long as we can get away with it.

Family, money, books, travel, food, shopping, binge watching, social media, love, independence, health, and work — these are just some of the things that bring people comfort.

Once again, many of these things are not inherently bad. But they all have one thing in common: they're temporary or short-lived in their ability to bring any kind of lasting comfort into our lives. That's why my heart was challenged when I came across verse 76 of Psalm 119. It goes like this:

May your unfailing love be my comfort, according to your promise to your servant. (NIV84)

The prayer of the Psalmist was that God's unfailing love would be his source of comfort. The more I thought about that the more I saw the wisdom in his request. The Psalmist had recognized the passing nature of so many things that bring us comfort in this life, so he prayed to God for his comfort to be founded in the *one* thing that would never fade, run out, or come to an end – the unfailing love of God.

You will also notice that this unfailing love from God was not just a pipe dream for the Psalmist. He correctly saw it as according to God's promise; and based upon that, he boldly asked that his comfort might be established.

There are so many wonderful things that God has given us in this life to bring us joy and comfort; and though they are our possessions here on earth, they were not meant to be our *eternal* possessions. For that we have the Lord, and Him alone.

In the beginning you laid the foundations of the earth, and the heavens are the work of your hands. They will perish, but you remain; they will all wear out like a garment. Like clothing you will change them and they will be discarded. But you remain the same, and your years will never end. (Psalm 102:25–27 NIV84)

Is hypnotism a safe practice for believers?

The Bible doesn't directly address hypnotism but that doesn't mean it has nothing to say on the subject. Here are the reasons I believe hypnotism is a bad idea:

To whom are you yielded? In a hypnotic session you must willingly yield to the suggestive influence of another human being. That alone ought to raise some red flags since believers are told over and over in God's Word to submit themselves to God (see James 4:7). In fact, our ultimate goal

98   PASTOR, I HAVE A QUESTION

is to be so completely yielded to the Holy Spirit that our hearts, minds, and bodies are submitted to God and God alone.

On whom are you depending? People turn to hypnotism because there's power in suggestion. But that power doesn't begin to compare to the power of God in the life of a believer. The Apostle Paul spoke of knowing Christ and the power of His resurrection (Philippians 3:10) as the passion of his life. Do Christians today know anything of that power? If we did, would we be turning to lesser powers like hypnotism?

What exactly are you battling? People turn to hypnotism to gain control, but over what? Is it not the flesh that people are wanting to conquer? As believers, we need to understand that any controlling aspect of the flesh in our lives really needs to be viewed as sin. And sin should only bring about one response from us — our need for the cross of Christ where we come to crucify the flesh. Paul wrote: "**I have been crucified with Christ. It is no longer I who live, but Christ who lives in me. And the life I now live in the flesh I live by faith in the Son of God**" (Galatians 2:20). This is the secret of the believer's freedom from the tyranny of the flesh and Paul declares it boldly in Romans 6 saying: "**We know that our old self was crucified with him in order that the body of sin might be brought to nothing, so that we would no longer be enslaved to sin. For one who has died has been set free from sin**" (vv. 6–7). Let's face it, we turn to things like hypnotism because we have no practical understanding of the power of the cross of Christ.

Hypnotism sets a precedent of self-focused problem-solving. What do you do when you have a problem? If you're like most Christians, you pray about it then you proceed to solve it in your own strength. Hypnotism is just another way of depending on myself to solve my own problems.

In his amazing autobiography, George Mueller warns against any attempt on our part to work our own deliverance. To do so is to *not* trust the Lord with all our heart, as we are encouraged to do (see Proverbs 3:5–6). Our focus should be on our Savior and not on anything else, and most definitely not on ourselves. We won't be able to find the answers within us. They're only found in Jesus Christ.

Galatians 5:22–23 reminds us that self-control is a fruit of the Holy Spirit whom we have freely received in Christ. As we follow the leading of God's Spirit, He promises to enable us to live our lives in a manner that brings Him glory. If there is an area of your life that is not bringing glory to God, the answer is to rely on the power our Lord has already given to meet that challenge.

Chapter 7

PRAYER

- When I pray, am I talking to God or Jesus? 101

- Is spoken prayer more powerful than a prayer expressed without words? 102

- God doesn't seem to be answering my prayers. What should I do? 103

- Since God is so powerful, do my prayers really make a difference? 105

- Can I oppose God's will through prayer? 106

- Are there ways to fast that don't involve abstaining from food? 107

- Why does Jesus teach us to ask forgiveness for our sins when He already secured our forgiveness on the cross? 109

- Why does Jesus teach us to pray, "lead us not into temptation?" 110

- Does God want me to use only the Hebrew names He was called in the Old Testament? 111

When I pray, am I talking to God or Jesus?

Whenever we deal with the nature of God, it's common for there to be a little confusion since God's nature is ultimately beyond our comprehension. Here are a couple things to keep in mind:

- The Bible reveals that God is **one** (Deuteronomy 6:4). That means there aren't two, three, or multiple Gods. There is only one God.

- As challenging as it is to grasp, the Bible also reveals that God has revealed Himself in three Persons: Father, Son, and Holy Spirit. They are distinct as Persons, but they are one in being.

That means when we refer to "God" it is impossible to separate the Father from the Son, or the Holy Spirit. They are one.

Jesus did teach us to pray saying, "Our Father, who is in heaven" (Matthew 6:9) and to pray "in my name" (John 16:26). But that doesn't literally mean that we're supposed to end our prayers with "In Jesus' name, Amen!" — although there's certainly nothing wrong with that.

To do something in another person's name means to do it as their representative, in their authority. Think of it like a key or access card. We come to the Father with the access to God that has been granted us by the sacrifice of Jesus. Therefore, when we approach God, we come in the authority and access of the Son of God.

I know this is a lot to think about. But keep in mind, there's nothing wrong with addressing *any* of the Persons of the Trinity separately. There are times when I pray saying, "Father, I come to You..." and other times when I address Jesus personally, or even the Holy Spirit. But regardless of the title or name that I'm using, I always know that I'm coming to God — and that means I'm coming to the Father, the Son and the Holy Spirit **together**.

Is spoken prayer more powerful than a prayer expressed without words?

I would have to say no for two reasons: First, there is *nothing* in the Word that directs us specifically to pray out loud as a means of making our prayers more effective. Second, there are biblical examples of prayers being offered up without words that were answered by the Lord.

One example is the prayer of Hannah, a woman who poured out her heart to God in prayer (see 1 Samuel 1). We are told that as she prayed, "only her lips moved, and her voice was not heard" (v. 13). And yet God powerfully answered her petition.

Nehemiah's is another example (see Nehemiah 2). He was tending to King Artaxerxes in his official role as cupbearer and during a conversation with the King, Nehemiah relates that he "prayed to the God of heaven" (v. 4) before answering a specific question that had been put to him by the king. Nehemiah hardly had time to go off and pray on his own, so it seems obvious from the text that he shot up a quick and silent prayer to the Lord his God, which was wonderfully answered.

Some believe the best passage in support of silent prayer

is 1 Thessalonians 5:17 where the Apostle Paul exhorts us to "pray without ceasing." This verse speaks of a constant and ongoing communication with God throughout our day, which would most certainly involve verbal and non-verbal petitions and thanksgiving.

We're clearly told in the Word that our heavenly Father knows what we need before we ask Him (Matthew 6:8). And yet He wants us to come to Him and pour out our needs before His throne of grace. There is certainly a place for verbal prayers and whenever possible, I try to pray out loud. Doing so gives me a greater sense of awareness that I am taking to my Lord. Obviously, that's not always possible. When voicing my prayers out loud isn't feasible, I move into silent prayer — confident that my Father in Heaven hears with equal clarity and eagerness.

God doesn't seem to be answering my prayers. What should I do?

Let's read the words of a man named George Mueller, who knew a little something about prayer:

In November, 1844, I began to pray for the conversion of five individuals. I prayed every day without a single intermission, whether sick or in health, on the land or on the sea, and whatever the pressure of my engagements might be. Eighteen months elapsed before the first of the five was converted. I thanked God and prayed on for the others. Five years elapsed, and then the second was converted. I thanked God for the second, and prayed on for the other three. Day by day I continued to pray for them, and six years passed before the third was converted. I thanked God for the three, and went on praying for the other two. These two remained unconverted... But I hope in God, I pray on, and look yet for the answer. They are not converted yet, but they will be.*

What an incredible man George Mueller was! He was no stranger to the place of prayer and was willing to wait on the Lord for answers. Mueller slipped into eternity in March of 1898, and at that time the last of the men for whom he had prayed — two sons of a friend of his youth — had not received Christ, even after 52 years of consistent daily petition.

But the story didn't end there. God, being full of mercy, re-membered the cries of his servant. Sometime after Mueller's death, the Lord graciously brought those two men "into the fold."

I share this because I believe it offers some much-needed insight to the idea of praying and waiting. So many times when we say that God doesn't seem to answer our prayer, what we should be saying is that He didn't answer according to the time frame of our expectations. Muller demonstrated the right posture of the heart Christians need to have and that is a never-give-up attitude toward prayer.

*Basil Miller, "George Muller: The Man of Faith and Miracles," *GeorgeMuller.org*, PDF.

Since God is so powerful, do my prayers really make a difference?

It's not possible *unless* we serve a God who can do anything — and that includes being able to determine the impact prayer will have on the direction and execution of His will. In other words, only a sovereign and all-powerful God can choose to allow the prayers of sinful human beings to have an impact on His determined will.

The problem with directing our focus on comprehending how God works among the sons of men is that we have a very limited ability to lay hold of His works. Even the Apostle Paul who understood a lot, had to stop and say:

Oh, the depth of the riches of the wisdom and knowledge of God! How unsearchable his judgments, and his paths beyond tracing out! "Who has known the mind of the Lord? Or who has been his counselor?" (Romans 11:33–34 NIV)

The simple answer is that it is beyond our ability to fathom *how* prayer works. Pastor Chuck Smith used to say that when we are faced with things we don't understand, we should fall back on what we *do* understand. So here's what we know about prayer. God's Word tells us: (1) **to pray** (2 Chronicles 7:14); that (2) **God will hear us** (2 Chronicles 7:14); and that (3) **prayer makes a difference** (James 5:16).

The details are bound up in the wisdom and majesty of God and for now, we will just need to leave it all there.

Can I oppose God's will through prayer?

The idea that a person can pray oneself out of the will of God is a diabolical thought that is sure to steal both the pleasure and the intimacy of prayer. God wants us to come to Him and pour out our hearts, and we can be sure that when we do, there will be times when we will utter things in prayer that are *not* in the perfect will of our Lord. We all do this. It's part of being an imperfect creature who sees "in a mirror dimly" (1 Corinthians 13:12). Jesus modeled for us the perfect prayer for such requests that may miss the mark of God's will. This is recorded for us in Matthew 26 where it says:

And going a little farther he fell on his face and prayed, saying, "My Father, if it be possible, let this cup pass from me; nevertheless, not as I will, but as you will..." (v. 39)

Did you notice how Jesus amended His request? He said, "**not as I will, but as you will.**"

This is the attitude in prayer that God would have us bring into all our petitions. Jesus included this instruction also in The Lord's Prayer when He told us to say, "**Your kingdom come, your will be done on earth as it is in heaven**" (Matthew 6:10).

We don't pray this way out of a fear that anything less will override the will of God in our lives, but rather we say it out of an attitude of *submission* that always desires to quickly and humbly kneel before the sovereign wisdom of our heavenly Father. This is the attitude that Jesus always modeled for us. This is outlined for us in the book of Hebrews where it says:

During the days of Jesus' life on earth, he offered up prayers and petitions with loud cries and tears to the one who could save him from death, and he was heard because of his reverent

submission. (Hebrews 5:7 NIV)

Don't ever let fear keep you from the place of prayer. Come before Him with confidence and lay down your petitions, understanding that He knows what you need even before you ask Him. And know this also that God has promised to lead you according to His will and He will *not* go back on that promise.

I will instruct you and teach you in the way you should go; I will counsel you with my eye upon you. (Psalm 32:8)

So when you pray, present your requests before the Lord with a heart of humility and submission, asking that God's will would sovereignly trump your own should you ever seek anything contrary to His plan.

And this is the confidence that we have toward him, that if we ask anything according to his will he hears us. (1 John 5:14)

Are there ways to fast that don't involve abstaining from food?

You don't have to read long in the Bible before coming across the idea of fasting. It may not always be mentioned by name, but the idea of focusing on God by withholding food (and in some cases even drink) is not an uncommon topic in the Word of God.

But did you know that there are other kinds of fasting? An example is fasting from sexual relations. In 1 Corinthians 7:5, the Apostle Paul speaks of married couples abstaining

108 PASTOR, I HAVE A QUESTION

from sexual relations for a short time in order to devote themselves to prayer. Even in the Old Testament, married couples in Israel were commanded to "fast" from sexual relations in preparation for meeting with the Lord on Mt. Sinai (Exodus 19:15).

I have found in my own experience that other kinds of fasting (abstaining from something other than food) have had a powerful impact on my devotional life. Every so often I feel led by the Lord to set something aside for a time so I can focus my heart and mind more pointedly on Him. I recall doing a month-long fast from Facebook and other online/television entertainment. That meant no movies or shows and no social media for that month. Only a few days into it, I could already feel the effects of detoxing from those time-sucking distractions. Instead of spending my time unwinding in front of the TV or my laptop, I spent it reading, writing, or just talking with my family. During that period of fasting, I really sensed a greater clarity of thought and attention to prayer and the Word.

We all need to be aware of the things that war against our spiritual progress and consider fasting from those things for a period of time. When I begin to sense a spiritual numbness, I know that nothing short of a time of fasting is going to fix the problem. Setting aside time to fast from things that would normally take my time and passion from the Lord always gets me excited and energized. I find myself looking forward to completing a period of fasting, as well as the renewed freedom to worship, pray, and study that comes as a result. This fasting stuff is way cool!

Why does Jesus teach us to ask forgiveness for our sins when He already secured our forgiveness on the cross?

When a person comes by faith to Jesus, accepts the sacrifice He made on the cross, and receives Him as Savior, that person is born again and completely forgiven of all sins — past, present, and future. This forgiveness is **for salvation** and it is perpetual (see 1 John 1:7).

Why then does the Bible tell us to come to the Lord and say, "Forgive us our trespasses" if we are already forgiven by the cross of Christ? It's for the sake of our **relationship with God**.

If you are a Christian — a believer and follower of Christ — you are in a relationship with God through His Son, and that relationship can easily get compromised and sullied by living in a world where sin is commonplace. This creates the need for us to come to the cross and find forgiveness so that no barriers exist between us and our Lord.

I'll use the analogy of marriage to explain our relationship with God and why we need to come to Him and regularly ask for forgiveness. My wife and I are married and our status as a married couple is perpetual. But because we have a close relationship, we sometimes do or say things that hurt the other person. When we do, we remain married, but there now exists a breach or rift in our relationship that needs to be mended before we can move on and be intimate once again. So we come together and confess our wrong attitudes, words, and actions, and we extend forgiveness where it is needed. In this way, the closeness of our relationship is restored through forgiveness. But throughout this process, our status as a married couple never changes.

In the same way, your relationship with God can easily become tainted and distant through sin. It doesn't mean you've lost your salvation or are no longer a child of God (that status cannot be affected by sin); but it *does* mean that sin affects your relationship with Him, and that relationship (closeness) needs to be restored. This is why we come to the Lord and confess our sins — so that nothing is able to create distance between us and our Lord.

This picture of cleansing is powerfully depicted in the foot washing that occurred during the Last Supper. Jesus explained, "**The one who has bathed does not need to wash, except for his feet, but is completely clean. And you are clean**..." (John 13:10). When we accept by faith the sacrifice of Jesus on the cross we are "completely clean." But the reality of everyday life causes us to occasionally need to wash our feet because we're walking every day through a world that is saturated with the filth of sin. Praise God that He has made a way for us to be cleansed every single day!

Why does Jesus teach us to pray, "lead us not into temptation?"

This petition basically expresses a healthy distrust of one's own ability to resist temptations or stand up under trial. It acknowledges that our dependence must be on the Lord to see us through.

The Greek word for *lead* carries the idea of "bringing inward." So the petition "**lead us not**" can be interpreted as essentially saying, "Do not allow us to be *carried inward* into temptation" or "Do not allow us to be carried away into temptation."

David prayed a similar prayer when he said, "**Do not let my heart incline to any evil, to busy myself with wicked deeds in company with men who work iniquity, and let me not eat of their delicacies!**" (Psalm 141:4).

Does God want me to use only the Hebrew names He was called in the Old Testament? Am I wrong to use titles like "God" or "Lord"?

The short answer to your question is *no*. You are not wrong to use the words "God" or "Lord" when speaking of God or when praying. Some people might object to this, reminding you that such words are just titles and not His true name. However, there's nothing at all wrong with titles. In His instructions to us about prayer, Jesus said:

Pray then like this: 'Our Father in heaven, hallowed be your name.' (Matthew 6:9)

We see here that Jesus specifically taught us to pray using the word "Father" which is also a title.

There has been a resurgence of interest in Hebrew language and culture among many Christians. In fact, there's been the emergence of an entire movement called "Hebrew Roots Movement" that has encouraged believers to learn more about Hebrew culture and language. Much of the desire to gain a better understanding of such things is good; however, I have seen this center of interest give rise to spiritual pride and become a path toward legalistic thinking and practices.

It's very easy to think that we have special access to God because we use the right words or refer to Him using a particular biblical name. But we need to remember that our access to God is through Jesus Christ and through Him alone. We're told in Matthew, Mark, and Luke that when Jesus died on the cross the veil in the temple was torn in two. That was God's way of showing us that the way into the Holy of Holies (His presence) had now been opened through the sacrifice of Jesus Christ. The Way, therefore, is *not* a name or a word or a title — it is a *Person*. Remember our Lord's words:

I am the way, and the truth, and the life. No one comes to the Father except through me. (John 14:6)

Chapter 8

MARRIAGE

- What does the Bible say about living together outside of marriage? 114

- What should you do when you realize you're married to an unbeliever? 117

- How should I respond if I am being discouraged by my husband to go to church? 120

- How do I respond to a husband who is sinning and won't admit it? 121

- What should be done in a Christian marriage when one spouse wants to tithe but the other doesn't? 124

- What is the marital position of a couple who are legally divorced but still living together? 126

- Where in the Bible does it say that a woman should take her husband's last name? 127

What does the Bible say about living together outside of marriage?

It would appear from the strong evidence of God's Word that a legitimate marriage is one in which two people have made a covenant (or binding agreement) to love and commit themselves to one another. (Biblically, such covenants were always made in front of witnesses.) An illegitimate marriage would be a union between a man and a woman where there has been no covenant and no commitment.

Scriptural Insights

These passages from the Bible speak of those who violate their marriage covenant:

[Wisdom] will save you also from the adulteress, from the wayward wife with her seductive words, who has left the partner of her youth and ignored the covenant she made before God. (Proverbs 2:16–17 NIV84)

In the passage above, the woman who engages in sexual activity outside of her marriage is called an "adulteress" and the Lord charges her with "ignoring the covenant she made before God." (Obviously, the Lord considers this a serious offense.)

...the LORD is acting as the witness between you and the wife of your youth, because you have broken faith with her, though she is your partner, the wife of your marriage covenant. (Malachi 2:14 NIV84)

In this passage, God speaks of the violation of a marriage covenant as "breaking faith" between two marriage partners.

These passages underscore the importance that God places upon a marriage covenant. But while we're shown here that

MARRIAGE   115

God recognizes and honors a marriage commitment, is there any evidence that living together outside of marriage is wrong – even when the couple has made a commitment of their own?

Below is a conversation that Jesus had with a woman who was living with a man outside of wedlock.

[Jesus] told her, "Go, call your husband and come back." "I have no husband," she replied. Jesus said to her, "You are right when you say you have no husband. The fact is, you have had five husbands, and the man you now have is not your husband. What you have just said is quite true." (John 4:16–18 NIV84)

This is a fascinating exchange because Jesus lovingly confronts the woman and uses her own words to confirm that the man she is currently living with is not her husband. In other words, Jesus did not recognize her "arrangement" as a true marriage, and therefore did not consider her live-in partner as her husband.

Once again, a marriage covenant is a promise made by a man and a woman before God, to love and care for one another. When this promise is given and witnessed (2 Corinthians 13:1), God considers the couple properly married and free to enjoy all the blessings and benefits of marriage. When a man and a woman refuse to come together under a marriage covenant, they are not considered properly married before God and are therefore in violation of God's Word.

Blessing or Judgment?
The writer of Hebrews said it this way:

Marriage should be honored by all, and the marriage bed kept pure, for God will judge the adulterer and all the sexually immoral. (Hebrews 13:4 NIV84)

116 PASTOR, I HAVE A QUESTION

In this single passage we're told that God honors the institution of marriage to such a degree that when an individual chooses to engage in sexual activity outside the boundaries of the marriage covenant, such activity will ultimately come under God's judgment. For Christians, this is a serious issue. As the Apostle Paul wrote, "It is God's will that you...should avoid sexual immorality; For God did not call us to be impure, but to live a holy life" (1 Thessalonians 4:3,7 NIV84).

Walking in Blessing

God greatly desires to bless your home, your marriage, and your life. As we surrender to the guidelines and wisdom of God's Word as recorded in the Bible, we open ourselves to that blessing in a wonderful way.

If you are currently in a situation where you are living with someone outside of a marriage commitment, I strongly encourage you to do one of two things: either move out immediately or make a commitment to the person with whom you are living and get married. (Remember, if you're a Christian and the other person is not, the best thing to do is to remain unmarried and celibate while you pray for their salvation and wait on the Lord.)

What should you do when you realize you're married to an unbeliever?

The saying "love is blind" is often true. The incredible rush of emotion that accompanies two people falling in love can cause us to ignore the warning signs and abandon our better judgment. We choose to believe the best about the person we want to marry and we ignore anything that might dissuade us from what our heart wants most.

So what do you do when you finally come to the realization that your spouse is most likely *not* a believer and shows little or no sign of wanting to change?

I'll begin by telling you something you *can't* do and that's getting a divorce. Having an unbelieving spouse does *not* qualify as biblical grounds for divorce, regardless of how antagonistic they may be about your faith. You married this person and committed yourself to them before the Lord. Now it's time to make good on your promise.

But here's the question the Apostle Paul would ask: *"Does your spouse still want to be married to you?"* He writes:

...if any brother has a wife who is an unbeliever, and she consents to live with him, he should not divorce her. If any woman has a husband who is an unbeliever, and he consents to live with her, she should not divorce him. (1 Corinthians 7:12–13)

These comments came about because some people in Paul's day had responded to the Gospel and trusted Christ while their spouses had not. They found themselves in a marriage that was divided on Christian grounds and they wanted to know what to do. Should they divorce their unbelieving spouse? Paul said no. If the unbelieving spouse had no problems remaining married, the believer was *not* to seek a divorce or a separation. Paul's advice was for them to remain married and committed.

But what if the unbelieving spouse was so repulsed by their partner's faith that they no longer wanted to remain in the marriage? Paul writes:

...if the unbelieving partner separates, let it be so. In such cases the brother or sister is not enslaved. God has called you to peace. (1 Corinthians 7:15)

The clear teaching here is that a believing husband or wife is not bound to the marriage if their spouse desires to leave and in fact does so.

Being married to an unbeliever can create challenges that you need to be aware of. Here are a few:

Prayerlessness. You cannot afford to stop praying. Being in a marriage that bears an unequal yoke requires you to daily bring your spouse, as well as your own heart, before the throne of grace. You will personally need God's grace and strength flowing constantly into your life to keep yourself from falling into all the other pitfalls listed below.

Manipulation. Realizing that you are spiritually alone in the relationship is likely to put you in a vulnerable position where you might be tempted to do and say all kinds of things to get your spouse into coming to church or reading the Bible. But these methods rarely produce fruit and most often cause the unbeliever to withdraw even further. Believers need to resist the temptation to beg, plead, or otherwise cajole their spouse into compliance with their wishes. Such manipulative actions are the opposite of trusting the Lord for your spouse's salvation.

MARRIAGE   119

Marital Independence. Sometimes when a Christian husband or wife finally accepts that their partner is an unbeliever, they will compensate for the spiritual vacuum in their marriage by throwing themselves into Bible studies and Christian service projects. These things could take up more and more of their time, to the point that they create a great distance between the husband and wife. This is usually a defense mechanism on the part of the Christian spouse, seeking to fill the void in their marriage with spiritual activity and busyness. Unfortunately, all this usually produces in the unbelieving partner is resentment which will not really warm them to the Gospel. When you're married to an unbeliever, you need to be careful to balance your time between your marriage and the Body of Christ.

Marital disappointment. The pain of being married to a spiritually disconnected spouse can become so severe that eventually the believer will surrender to disappointment. The negative emotions that result can be leveled at their spouse or even at God. Either way, it has a destructive and very spiritually corrosive effect.

Steering clear of these pitfalls will come as you stay firmly and consistently connected to the Body of Christ and keep your heart fed with the Word of God. Your challenges are admittedly difficult, but the Lord will be your strength and He will encourage you along the way. Remember this — you are the believer in the family and as such, God will give you opportunities to bring the life of Jesus into the relationship and the enabling grace to keep bringing your spouse before Him in prayer.

How should I respond if I am being discouraged by my husband to go to church?

Living with a spouse who is antagonistic toward your Christian faith can be hurtful and very challenging to deal with. Here are some things to keep in mind:

Walk in respect
Peter wrote specifically to women concerning how to respond in difficult situations with a husband. He said:

...wives, be subject to your own husbands, so that even if some do not obey the word, they may be won without a word by the conduct of their wives, when they see your respectful and pure conduct. (1 Peter 3:1–2)

Think and pray on these words and ask the Lord how best to apply them in your home and with your husband. God will give you the guidance you need.

Consider your options
As far as going to church, there are lots of ways today to make sure you're connecting with the Body of Christ and staying spiritually nourished. Hebrews 10:25 tells us not to forsake the assembling of ourselves together with others, but *when* that fellowship takes place is not all that important. In other words, if your husband objects to you being away on Sunday morning, consider another day or time to meet with believers. I would encourage you to contact your local church and see if they offer any Bible studies or women's groups that meet at times that would work better for you.

Online
Staying in the Word and keeping up your spiritual strength is very important. Many pastors, myself included, have studies

through the entire Bible available for you to access anytime. Keep yourself nourished and encouraged while you continue to pray for your husband and wait on the Lord.

How do I respond to a husband who is sinning and won't admit it?

I caught him lying to me recently concerning the pornographic movies he watched while I was on vacation. How am I expected to deal with lying and deception? I am angry and I do not know how to process this in a godly manner.

I'm sorry for your situation. I can certainly understand your anger and frustration, and I'm very glad you're desiring to handle this situation in a godly way.

The first thing I want to make very clear is that you're dealing with your husband and not your son. That may seem like an obvious remark, but oftentimes I find that when wives are confronted with poor behavior by their husbands, they convert to "mom mode." That means they treat their husbands in the same manner they would address problematic behavior with a child. It usually ends very badly for both husband and wife.

I mention this because you are called by God to show respect for your husband, and that calling is not set aside just because your husband is acting badly. In other words, the exhortation for wives to respect their husbands is not expected of you only when your husband is *deserving* of respect — you are called to respect him at *all* times. That doesn't mean you have to just be quiet and put up with his bad behavior. It means that when you address these matters with him, you need to do so with respect.

There are many people, including Christians, who believe that when a husband does the kinds of things your husband has done, he is no longer deserving of respect. When you look at it exclusively from the standpoint of his actions, that certainly seems to be the case. But as a Christian, you must also view this matter through the lenses of God's Word. And rarely is obedience to God's Word ever going to be convenient — your situation is a perfect example.

I'm not at all surprised that when you confronted your husband, he lied to you. Individuals who engage in pornography live in a world of darkness and intense shame. Admitting that there is a problem is extremely hard, and even more so when admitting it to someone who will be deeply hurt by it. Deep down your husband knows what he's doing is wrong, and because he's a man, he wants to appear strong to you. When you confronted him, you forced him to expose a very weak and ugly part of his life. His refusal to acknowledge it means he desperately wants to avoid appearing weak in your eyes.

So how should you respond? I would like to list five ways I believe the Lord would have you respond to your husband:

Respectfully. As I've already pointed out, the calling of a wife is to respect her husband — even when he's struggling. Ask the Lord to help you with this by giving you the words to say and by reminding you of the words you shouldn't say.

Prayerfully. This is not a time to neglect the practice of prayer. You need to be praying for your husband, that the Lord would convict him of his sin and that he would reach out for support from other men. Also pray for yourself and for your marriage. Ask the Lord to give you strength and discernment as to how best to act and respond. Pray for God's peace in the midst of it all.

Biblically. Peter addressed the very situation you are going through in his first letter. Read 1 Peter 3:1–6 and ask the Lord to show you how that passage applies to your situation.

Confidently. It can be a *very* fearful thing when a woman gives herself to the leadership of a man, only to discover that he is not leading as he should. The resulting fear can propel a woman to respond in many ways, some of which can be just as damaging to the marriage as her husband's behavior and therefore, the need for caution is very real. Put your trust firmly in your Savior. Though people disappoint you, Jesus will never forsake you or let you down. Put your confidence in the Lord's grace and power.

Confidentially. When you're angry, the thought of protecting someone who has hurt you is hard to wrap your head around, but be cautious with whom you share this matter. Your husband *does* need help, but it's not going to come about through the humiliation brought on by being publicly exposed. You want him to be restored, not crushed and defeated.

I want to end by reminding you that your main question centered around what *you* should do about this matter, and not what your husband should do. I have endeavored to be faithful to that focus. (I thought it would be pointless to tell you what your husband needs to do.) And although you can't control your husband, you *can* pray for him – and that is an option you can't afford to neglect.

What should be done in a Christian marriage when one spouse wants to tithe but the other doesn't?

Please forgive me if this sounds sexist, but it depends on whether the person wanting to tithe is the husband or the wife. And frankly, it's not sexist at all, because within the context of marriage God has given each partner some very specific roles. For the man, there is a role of headship so if he is the one wanting to tithe, he should be prepared to sit down with his wife to discuss with her the subject of giving from a standpoint anchored in God's Word and explain to her why it's a biblical idea.

Even then, the last thing a husband wants to do is force his wife into giving against her will. (Remember, God wants a willing heart.) If she is still reluctant about giving, it behooves the husband to discover the reasons behind why his wife is feeling that way and encourage and pray for her accordingly.

If, however, the husband is the one who is resistant to the idea of giving, the wife needs to earnestly come to the Lord in prayer, asking God to change her husband's heart. 1 Peter 3:1–2 is the passage a wife needs to follow in this case. Meanwhile and until her husband responds to the Lord, she should consider other ways she can give to the Lord (apart from giving financially). The last thing a wife should do is nag him about it, or worse yet, give without his consent.

Let me end with one last comment on the matter of tithing. The word "tithe" literally means ten percent, and it first appears in the Hebrew Scriptures which we call the Old Testament. Tithing was demanded of the Israelites as part of the Law, and while the idea of giving is still very much present in the New Testament, the specifics have somewhat changed. Instead of God requiring ten percent, believers in Jesus are asked to give whatever they have determined in their hearts to give. Paul expounded on this in 2 Corinthians 9:7 when he wrote:

Each of you should give what you have decided in your heart to give, not reluctantly or under compulsion, for God loves a cheerful giver. (NIV)

Why is there no more command to give ten percent, you ask? It's because under the new covenant, those numbers have changed. We now owe Jesus *one hundred percent* of our lives. As the Apostle Paul wrote:

You are not your own. You were bought at a price. (1 Corinthians 6:19b–20a NIV)

Jesus purchased us completely by His death on the cross and that means you now belong entirely to Him. Everything you are and everything you own is His. And yet, even so, He graciously allows you the freedom to give whatever is in your heart to give. That is why Paul encourages us to give cheerfully.

What is the marital position of a couple who are legally divorced but still living together?

Marriage is a covenant of love and faithfulness that is promised and kept between a man and a woman. It is a sharing of all that we are and all that we have — a joining of two lives, so intimate that God refers to the two as "**one flesh**" (Genesis 2:24).

There have been many couples over the years who have signed a marriage license but never lived as if they were married. Such marriages of convenience are usually entered into to take advantage of legal or financial considerations. But in some cases, the couple never lived together or shared anything that involved having normal marital relations. Are they married in God's eyes? I hardly think so. A state-issued license does not make a marriage.

Now let's look at a couple that comes together in love and mutual commitment to share their lives with one another in marriage. Somewhere along the way they decided to divorce and go through all the legal requirements for ending their marriage in the eyes of the state — yet they remain together physically and emotionally.

From a biblical standpoint, I believe this couple is still married in God's eyes. The only place their marriage has ended is in the realm of the state which means there are certain benefits they no longer have a legal right to enjoy.

As the Creator of the marriage union, God has established His own guidelines for determining who is married and who is not. And His Word makes it clear that only death or unfaithfulness (adultery or desertion by an unbeliever) can end a marriage (see Romans 7:2; Matthew 5:31–32; 1 Corinthians 7:10–15). That means God does *not* check the legal records at the courthouse to see if a couple is married or divorced.

Where in the Bible does it say that a woman should take her husband's last name?

Nowhere. A woman taking her husband's last name in marriage is a tradition, not a biblical command. There is nothing in the Bible about this tradition because in biblical times most people didn't have last names. They were identified by the area in which they lived (i.e., Jesus of Nazareth) or by their spouse (i.e., Joanna, the wife of Chuza) or even by their birth father (i.e., James the son of Alphaeus).

The custom of a woman taking the name of her husband comes more from Western culture and tradition and therefore there's nothing inherently biblical in the practice. By the same token, there's nothing inherently unbiblical if a woman chooses to maintain her maiden name or even use both her maiden name and her husband's name.

Taking someone's last name in marriage is far less important than truly understanding what God intends for two people when they come together in marriage. God refers to a married couple as "one flesh" (Genesis 2:24) which speaks of an incredible intimacy and oneness. The sharing of a surname is one way of identifying that a man and a woman have entered that union.

Chapter 9

SPIRITUAL GIFTS

- How do I discover my spiritual gifts? 129

- Should all believers have the gift of tongues? 131

- Are personal words of prophecy (i.e., messages "from the Lord") biblical? 132

- Can we trust people who claim to have the ability to see our future? 134

How do I discover my spiritual gifts?

I have five tips for discovering your spiritual gift:

1. Understand what the Bible says about spiritual gifts.

I would encourage studying and being thoroughly familiar with 1 Corinthians 12, 13 and 14. These chapters not only talk about spiritual gifts but also address motives and the orderly use of such gifts. Also study Romans 12.

2. Ask the Lord to reveal your spiritual gift and trust that He will do it.

Spiritual gifts are given by God (see 1 Corinthians 12:4–7) therefore, you need to spend time praying that God would reveal your spiritual gift. But be very careful about putting an expiration date on your prayer. Most of us start praying with predetermined expectations about when God should give us an answer. Don't give God a deadline. Wait patiently and don't allow yourself to give in to frustration while waiting. Waiting is never easy, but God's timing is best.

3. Be open to the empowering work of the Holy Spirit.

Spiritual gifts are empowered by the Spirit of God. Never forget that. Pray that God would empower you with His Holy Spirit and be open to whatever manifestations of the Spirit He wishes to grant you. Read through the book of Acts and note the times that God's servants were filled with the Holy Spirit and enabled to do what would have otherwise been impossible.

4. Get busy serving in your local church.

In my case, my spiritual gift was discovered as I just got busy serving. My local church needed some helpers in the youth ministry and Sue and I helped in whatever way we could. Eventually the ministry leader left, and we were given the leadership reins for the youth, and I was thrust into sharing the Word. Not only did I discover that I loved it, but I came to realize that God had bestowed on me a spiritual gift that He wanted me to keep using to encourage His people.

You may have some areas of ministry in your local church that are hit and miss, but that's okay. Learning where you are not gifted can be just as important. Stick with it and keep opening your heart to new possibilities and opportunities.

5. Be faithful as you wait.

The Lord may have you in an area of ministry that isn't your favorite, but He may just want to see if you're willing to be faithful. Remember the life of Joseph in the book of Genesis (particularly in chapters 39 and 40). Faithfulness is everything, so stick with it and continue to trust God to reveal your spiritual gift. Do what you're given to do and follow this exhortation: *Whatever you do, work heartily, as for the Lord and not for men, knowing that from the Lord you will receive the inheritance as your reward. You are serving the Lord Christ* (Colossians 2:23–24).

Should all believers have the gift of tongues?

Instructions concerning the spiritual gift of speaking in tongues appear in just one of Paul's New Testament letters. In 1 Corinthians 12, Paul writes:

Are all apostles? Are all prophets? Are all teachers? Do all work miracles? Do all possess gifts of healing? Do all speak with tongues? Do all interpret? But earnestly desire the higher gifts. (vv. 29–31)

In these verses, the Apostle asks a series of rhetorical questions, each of which assumes a negative response. No, not everyone is called to be an apostle; no, not everyone has a prophetic gifting; no, not everyone is a teacher, and so on. The same is true with the gift of tongues – not everyone is so gifted.

However, there are certain groups within Christianity that have either decided to ignore what the Apostle writes here, or believe he is saying something other than what appears obvious to the rest of us. Either way, some have linked the gift of tongues to salvation in such a way as to require it as proof that a person has been genuinely saved. This teaching is not only unbiblical but also dangerous.

Having said that, let me be very quick to say that spiritual gifts are *not* dangerous. There is an attitude of "guilty by association" in the minds of many believers who make an unfortunate connection between the unbiblical use of spiritual gifts and the gifts themselves. This is incredibly sad on many levels. The fact is, spiritual gifts come to us through the agency of the Holy Spirit. To believe that our Lord could ever bring us anything that is not for our good and not for building up the Kingdom of God is unthinkable.

I believe the Apostle Paul's exhortation that begins 1 Corinthians 14 is just as important today as it was when he wrote it:

Pursue love, and earnestly desire spiritual gifts... (v. 1)

Are personal words of prophecy (i.e., messages "from the Lord") biblical?

What you're describing concerning personal prophecy is called a "word of knowledge" or a "word of wisdom." The Apostle Paul talks about these gifts in 1 Corinthians 12. We also see these gifts operational in the book of Acts.

Such prophetic utterances are very biblical, but they are also greatly abused in the Body of Christ today. I am very wary of receiving a prophetic word from anyone I don't know or anyone who doesn't have a proven track record of maturity and prophetic sensitivity.

We are called to "not believe every spirit, but test the spirits to see whether they are from God" (1 John 4:1) and this exhortation especially includes prophetic messages. Here are some ways we can test such things:

- **Through the inner witness of the Spirit.** Does the message resonate in my heart as true? Does it give me a check in my spirit — that uneasy, unsettling feeling of alarm or discomfort?

SPIRITUAL GIFTS   133

- ***Through the Word of God.*** Is there anything in the message that violates what I know to be true in the Bible?

- ***Through the test of time.*** If the message spoken to me was about something that "will happen" in the future, did that event actually come to pass just as the message said it would?

- ***Through prayer.*** We should always pray about any personal message that is supposed to have come from the Lord and I would encourage you to ask Him to confirm it through other sources. If God is speaking to you, He doesn't mind repeating Himself for the sake of clarity and confirmation.

Anyone who becomes annoyed or angry when we tell them we will test their message to see if it holds up is not operating in the Holy Spirit and should be avoided. Not everyone who claims to have a message from the Lord is truly walking in the Spirit.

Prophetic messages are a wonderful way for the Lord to encourage or warn us, but we must be diligent to test everything.

Can we trust people who claim to have the ability to see our future?

There is such a thing as the gift of prophecy and sometimes those so gifted may have something revealed to them from the Lord about what is to come — whether a future event or a future action by someone or a group of people.

In the Bible there are many examples of God allowing His prophets to know what would come to pass in the days ahead. But those insights were given so that the prophet could sound a warning to individuals or to an entire nation. Let me repeat, prophets themselves cannot know the future without God revealing it to them. They have no power within themselves to see what is to come.

Along with those who have a genuine prophetic gifting, the Bible also warns about false prophets. Jesus said, "**Beware of false prophets, who come to you in sheep's clothing but inwardly are ravenous wolves**" (Matthew 7:15). The Apostle John encouraged us in a similar way, saying, "**Beloved, do not believe every spirit, but test the spirits to see whether they are from God, for many false prophets have gone out into the world**" (1 John 4:1).

Notice that John tells us to "**test the spirits**" — this means to test any prophetic messages we may receive. We test them by comparing what they are saying to Scripture, and by allowing the test of time to play out to see if what they are saying comes to pass.

And finally, we test the prophet's own personal "fruit" meaning, their way of life. Jesus said, "**You will recognize them by their fruits**" (Matthew 7:16). Anyone with a true prophetic gifting will be humble and welcome this kind of testing. False prophets, on the other hand, will demand that you accept their words at face value and become annoyed if you insist on putting them to the test.

If you are currently in an environment where people are often claiming to know the future life and actions of others, I would encourage you to be very cautious and perhaps even find a new fellowship. Although prophetic giftings are biblical and real, false prophets are just as real.

Chapter 10

WHAT DOES THE BIBLE SAY ABOUT...

- Is it biblical for a woman to be a pastor? 138

- Is forgiving oneself a biblical concept? 140

- What does the Bible say about generational curses? 141

- What does the Bible say about cremation? 144

- What does the Bible say about alcohol and is it okay for Christians to partake? 145

- Is there anything in God's Word that forbids a believer to get a tattoo? 147

- What does the Bible say about men wearing feminine clothing and vice versa? 149

- How can Christians make sense of all the gender confusion in the world? 150

- What does the Bible say about race? How can we combat racism? 151

WHAT DOES THE BIBLE SAY ABOUT... 137

- Is there a verse or passage I can use to convince people that a fetus is a human being? 153

- Are women required to wear head coverings today? 154

- Is wearing jewelry a sin? 155

- Does the Bible tell us to confess our sins to everyone? 157

- Am I rejecting God by going to the doctor and taking medicine? 160

- Is getting a vaccine an act of unbelief? 163

- Does the Bible forbid Christian business owners from providing services to homosexuals? 164

- Is Christmas a holiday with pagan roots? 165

- What does God say about a believer taking a life, e.g., capital punishment or killing in defense? 168

- Can Christians be involved in political affairs? 170

- Is civil disobedience biblical? 171

Is it biblical for a woman to be a pastor?

I appreciate the fact that you specifically asked to hear what the Bible has to say on this subject. (Too often I'm asked for my own opinion.)

There are no references in God's Word pointing to women attaining the position of pastor or leader of a fellowship. There are people who believe that: (1) the absence of women pastors in biblical times is due to the low status of women at the time; and that (2) there is a need to revise such ideas and allow women to serve alongside men in the pastoral calling. I respect this view, but I think that this position is subject to scrutiny in light of the following question:

Is the absence of women pastors in the Bible just a reflection of society in biblical times, or are there genuine scriptural reasons which transcend culture and time that support this position?

It's just too easy to dismiss biblical ideas as "outdated" or merely cultural. I'm going to go out on a limb and say that I believe there *is* solid biblical ground for not having women function in the traditional role as pastor — reasons that have *nothing* whatsoever to do with equality or ability.

One thing I want to make clear at the outset is that I believe women to be capable of functioning in a pastoral role in every way. In fact, I have observed that in some cases, women can do a better job than their male counterparts when it comes to many aspects of leadership. My own wife is a very capable leader in her own right, excelling in areas including teaching and administrative oversight.

So, why then do I believe that women ought not to function as pastors of a fellowship? One of the key passages comes in a statement made by the Apostle Paul in his first letter to Timothy when he said:

I do not allow a woman to teach or to exercise authority over a man... (1 Timothy 2:12 NASB)

Here's the real question: Did the Apostle Paul make this statement because he was influenced by his own patriarchal society, or was he being led by the Holy Spirit? I believe it's the latter, and the reason I believe he said this was to protect the foundation of the home and family.

The Bible reveals that God has placed an order in Creation between men and women. It is communicated this way:

For the husband is the head of the wife as Christ is the head of the church, his body, of which he is the Savior. (Ephesians 5:23 NIV)

It is vital to note that the order within a husband-and-wife relationship has absolutely nothing to do with equality, intelligence, or ability. The Bible does *not* teach that men are superior and women are inferior. Now you might ask, "Why did God decide to give this role of 'headship' to the man?" That's a good question because I have observed that women often make better leaders. But what we *do* know is that this pattern of headship is one which reflects the very relationship of Christ to the Church. If you analyze the passage from Ephesians quoted above, you'll notice the connection.

Therefore, just as it would be inappropriate for the Church to instruct its Head (Jesus Christ), it is likewise inappropriate for a wife to instruct her husband. Why? Because the moment she does, she becomes the one assuming the role of headship, not her husband. And this is a violation of God's created order.

Keep in mind that although the title "pastor" is never ascribed to a woman in Scripture, it doesn't mean that a woman cannot function in a pastoral role. To *pastor* is to *shepherd*. (In fact, the same Greek word is translated as both "pastor" and "shepherd.") And women are encouraged to minister in this way: to shepherd, encourage, and instruct women in the Word of God (see Ephesians 5:23).

Is forgiving oneself a biblical concept?

Self-forgiveness is a derivative of the secular belief that you can't love others until you learn to love yourself (which is untrue, by the way). On a Christian level the idea has been transferred over to essentially say that you can't forgive others until you've forgiven yourself.

The problem is, this idea has absolutely *no* biblical foundation.

The whole concept of self-forgiveness is a creation of modern Western thinking that is accustomed to viewing all things through the looking glass of *self*. Living in the "selfie culture," it's normal for us to see ourselves at the center of every event of our lives. Wherever we go or whatever we do, there we find the "me, myself, and I" as the focus of the camera, with all else comfortably in the background. It's just the way we've learned to view life and we see nothing strange about it. But it *is* strange, and damaging too.

For us believers, the Holy Spirit is constantly working to draw us away from a "me-centered" existence and toward a life where Jesus Christ takes center stage. His thoughts ought to increasingly become our thoughts, and His truth ought to transform and renew the way we believe and think. When He tells us we are forgiven, we need to adjust our thinking accordingly. He is the Master, and His determination of our lives should trump our own thoughts every time. To say, "But I haven't forgiven myself!" is to elevate our own opinion and feelings above His and it only reveals an attitude of self-importance. We need to meditate on Galatians 2:20 which says:

I have been crucified with Christ. It is no longer I who live, but Christ who lives in me. And the life I now live in the flesh I live by faith in the Son of God, who loved me and gave himself for me.

What does the Bible say about generational curses?

I've had a fair number of people ask me this question. Some variations to the question include: *"How can I break a generational curse?" "Is my family under a generational curse?" "Is it because of a generational curse that bad things are happening to me?" "Could it be that a generational curse is the reason I am unable to get past some areas of sin in my life?"*

Let me begin by citing the passage from which the belief in "generational curses" has emerged:

You shall not bow down to them or serve them; for I the Lord your God am a jealous God, visiting the iniquity of the fathers on the children to the third and fourth generation of those who

142 PASTOR, I HAVE A QUESTION

hate me... (Deuteronomy 5:9)

A great many Christians have been taught about generational curses from this passage. They have been told that an ongoing curse from the Lord may be happening in their lives because of the past sins of family members. This has given rise to complex strategies on how to break generational curses. Many people have also embraced the belief that generational curses are to be blamed for anything bad that may be happening in their lives.

But is that what the passage is saying? No.

The reason so many stumble here is because they ignore the five critical words found at the very end of the verse — "**of those who hate me.**" This passage teaches us that God visits the iniquity of the fathers upon the sons to the third and fourth generation *of those who hate Him*. In other words, the children are carrying on what the parents started — a hatred and rejection of God. This is the reason why the judgment continues "to the third and fourth generation."

But what about those who repent of their sin and come to Christ? Are they still under the Lord's judgment for the former sins of their parents or grandparents?

There is a fundamental truth that all Christians need to learn and accept — **generational judgments are broken when we repent of sin and turn to Jesus in faith**. Coming to Jesus in faith breaks every chain. Jesus is the One who *sets us free* from every tie to the past. That is why the Apostle Paul wrote, "**Therefore, if anyone is in Christ, he is a new creation. The old has passed away; behold, the new has come**" (2 Corinthians 5:17). This statement would be categorically false if generational judgments are still in place for those who have put their faith in Jesus.

WHAT DOES THE BIBLE SAY ABOUT... 143

The Bible declares that you are a new creation! Do you know what that means? It means your past — even the horrific things done by you or your relatives, even strongholds of sin — cannot control or dominate you any longer. As Jesus declared, **"if the Son sets you free, you will be free indeed"** (John 8:36).

But be careful here. Being set free from your past by Jesus doesn't mean you're no longer able to live in sin once again. There's no longer anything compelling you to live that way, but you can still choose to do so. That's why the Apostle Paul wrote what he did to the Galatians when he said, **"For freedom Christ has set us free; stand firm therefore, and do not submit again to a yoke of slavery"** (Galatians 5:1). Jesus has set you free from the chains of your past, so you no longer have to live a life of slavery to your sinful impulses. But that doesn't mean you can't choose to return to that place of slavery. Sadly, some people do.

I hear Christians saying: *"This stronghold of sin has taken control of my life,"* or *"This is why divorce is rampant in my family."* Still others say: *"We have a spirit of anger over our family,"* or *"We're all struggling with a spirit of fear and that's why anxiety remains an issue in our family."*

They say such things as if there's no power in the Gospel — no overcoming victory in the cross. And yet, the Bible says that we are "more than conquerors" through Christ (Romans 8:37). I sometimes wonder, *how many Christians are living in the defeat of their family's sinful past?* How many are still enslaved to a purposeless existence that is robbed of the joy that ought to be theirs in Christ Jesus?

I've got news for you. If you're in Christ, you are a new creation! You've been birthed into a new family with an entirely new family identity. This new identity — and not your family's sinful past — is what controls your life. The Bible declares that we are "**from God and have overcome**...**for he who is in you is greater than he who is in the world**" (1 John 4:4). Greater is He that is in you *now* than the old self that controlled you in the past.

You have a new "family likeness" not founded on the patterns of family-related sins but rather on the Person of Jesus Christ. Just respond with a heart of faith to what the Bible tells you about your new life in Christ and boldly declare, *"I am no longer bound to my past or the past of my family. I am free in Christ to follow a new Master — Jesus Christ my Lord."*

What does the Bible say about cremation?

I can tell you confidently that the Bible says nothing about cremation. In fact, there is an absence of any kind of instruction concerning burial practices in Scripture. Instead, the Bible simply reveals how other cultures, such as the Jews, buried their dead. And although this is described for us in several biblical narratives, these things were never given as instructions or directives on how we ought to do it.

Some people are uncomfortable with cremation because of the fact that it was not practiced as a burial option in the Bible. But if you study the Scriptures closely, you'll find that our modern forms of burial are also not mentioned there.

Another reason some believers express misgivings about cremation is their concern about the resurrection to come. They say that if their body is nothing but ash, there will be nothing for God to raise. But this reasoning fails to take into account the fact that many of the bodies of the saints have turned to dust long ago and that there were also others who surrendered their bodies to the flames of martyrdom — and yet those people are no less in line for a new resurrection body than anyone else. There is not one single biblical passage that declares to us that a body burned in fire cannot or will not be raised incorruptible.

What does the Bible say about alcohol and is it okay for Christians to partake?

The Bible does not denounce all drinking of alcohol, but it passionately condemns drunkenness. The Bible contains many warnings against "strong drink" as well as narratives of ill-fated outcomes as a result of unrestrained drinking. A good example of a biblical warning concerning drinking says:

Wine is a mocker, strong drink a brawler, and whoever is led astray by it is not wise. (Proverbs 20:1)

Is it right that some Christians drink?
As much as some would like me to give a one-size-fits-all response to this question, I cannot. The question itself stems from a faulty premise which highlights alcohol as being bad or evil. It is *not*. The human heart is the evil component in this equation, often producing a troubling lack of control. That, along with the potentially devastating effects of alcohol, have produced untold suffering and heartache in people's lives for countless centuries. It would be exceedingly foolish to fail to take into consideration all the needless pain

146 PASTOR, I HAVE A QUESTION

that the simple act of drinking alcohol has caused. But let me reiterate: Alcohol is *not* the villain here — it is the sinful heart of man that fails to see danger when it presents itself. And to such a heart, alcohol brings a boatload of potential hazard.

So, rather than say "this is right" or "that is wrong," let me instead say that drinking alcohol is potentially unwise for the vast majority of people. The chances of being led astray by alcohol are pretty high and anyone who refuses to recognize that possibility is a fool in light of the Bible's many warnings. The book of Proverbs reminds us, "The prudent sees danger and hides himself, but the simple go on and suffer for it" (22:3). Alcohol coupled with the human heart is one big danger zone that I believe is best to avoid.

For those Christians who feel the liberty to drink on occasion, I have a few questions: *Are you aware that others are watching how you live? Are you also aware that some of those who are watching are not free to do what you do and would be quickly overcome if they were to follow your example?*

I have to confess that my heart is grieved when I see Christians raising a glass of some alcoholic beverage in pictures plastered all over social media. This reckless lack of concern for their weaker brothers and sisters in Christ is both shocking and saddening. If you are one who feels the freedom to drink, let me remind you that you do not have the freedom to cause your brother in Christ to stumble. The Apostle Paul said, "**It is good not to...drink wine or do anything that causes your brother to stumble**" (Romans 14:21). Caring for others ought to come before the exercise of your freedom.

Is there anything in God's Word that forbids a believer to get a tattoo?

Nothing, really. People love to quote Leviticus 19:28 which says: "You shall not make any cuts on your body for the dead or tattoo yourselves: I am the LORD."

But this prohibition was centered around forbidding the Israelites to mimic the worship practices of their pagan neighbors. It doesn't necessarily translate to a prohibition on Christians from getting a tattoo since modern tattoos are not connected with pagan worship practices.

So, how should Christians deal with this matter?

I think 1 Corinthians 6:19–20 is a good starting point for us to know some of the most important things we need to consider. Paul says:

Do you not know that your body is a temple of the Holy Spirit, who is in you, whom you have received from God? You are not your own; you were bought at a price. Therefore honor God with your body. (NIV84)

The first consideration every Christian ought to have concerning a tattoo is whether the Lord has given the go-ahead. According to the passage above, your body no longer belongs to you. It's God's — bought and paid for by His blood and therefore, you need to make sure He's okay with it.

Secondly, any consideration for a tattoo needs to be in keeping with the exhortation to "honor God with your body." Is the tattoo something that will bring honor to the Lord?

Finally, Christians are to be influenced by the Word, not the world. If your motivation for getting a tattoo is simply

148 PASTOR, I HAVE A QUESTION

because it's popular, then you might want to reconsider your decision. As a believer, you are to be led by the Spirit of Christ, not the spirit of the world.

I understand that these comments don't touch on the issue of someone who's had a tattoo which they now regret. It's not uncommon for an individual to come to Christ after having received one or more tattoos of questionable or even objectionable content. In that case, what do they do?

The feeling you get when looking at a tattoo that only reminds you of your foolish past is probably similar to how the Apostle Paul felt at his recollection of his own life before Christ. That life wasn't something he was proud of, and he even wrote to the Corinthians about it saying:

For I am the least of the apostles, unworthy to be called an apostle, because I persecuted the church of God. (1 Corinthians 15:9)

But this statement wasn't meant as an expression of self-regret or self-disappointment. Instead, Paul's past was a vivid reminder to him of the grace that had been shown him and his new calling as an apostle. Paul knew that he wasn't worthy of God's love and attention and he certainly wasn't worthy of his position in God's Kingdom. His past only underscored that truth — and continually reminded him of the depth and beauty of God's unlimited grace.

What does the Bible say about men wearing feminine clothing and vice versa?

The definition of "feminine" and "masculine" when it comes to clothing is constantly changing. God's Word does address what we would call "cross-dressing," (see Deuteronomy 22:5) but clothing styles have changed drastically since biblical times so it's impossible to say women should wear this and men should wear that.

We need to be careful not to narrow down the issue to trivial matters like whether it's better for women to wear dresses than shirts and pants, or for men to wear jeans instead of shorts. What God is *most* concerned about is the heart. He created the two genders to be fundamentally different and it is a departure from God's creative order for us to blur the lines in any way (clothing included).

When God addresses the issue of men wearing clothing traditionally worn by women, He is addressing the heart of man first and foremost. Man's unwillingness to submit to God's gender distinctions is just another act of rebellion and wickedness on man's part, and God condemns all acts of rebellion against His creative order.

How can Christians make sense of all the gender confusion in the world?

It's true, there's a boatload of confusion in our world today concerning gender. From what I've read, you are now presented with a bewildering list of gender identities to choose from when you create a new Facebook account. Reading through the quagmire of gender options, it becomes very clear that people genuinely believe gender is something you can choose as you would your clothing.

Understanding gender from the perspective of God's Word isn't confusing at all. In fact, the Bible is very straightforward on the subject:

God created man in his own image, in the image of God he created him; male and female he created them. (Genesis 1:27)

There you have it, God made two genders — male and female. So, where did all this gender uncertainty come from? Simple answer: the darkened and rebellious heart of man.

Ever since the corrupting influence of sin entered the human race, mankind has been in open rebellion against God and His sovereign rule. The Lord our God decreed in the beginning that mankind is "male and female" but the sons of Adam will have none of it. "No!" he shouts, shaking his fist in the air, "We refuse to submit to God and the distinctions He set on gender!" Man then sets out to recreate the world in his own distorted image.

This rebellion on the part of mankind is powerfully expressed in the Psalms:

The kings of the earth take their stand and the rulers gather together against the Lord and against his Anointed One. "Let us break their chains," they say, "and throw off their fetters." (Psalm 2-3 NIV84)

All this talk of alternate expressions of sexuality and transgenderism is nothing more than man throwing off what he considers to be the shackles of God's sovereign rule. Man refuses to be ruled by God and he chafes under what he sees as God's unfair dominion. Mankind desires above all else to be his own ruler — free to live as he deems right. Just as it was said of the nation of Israel in the time of the Judges, "**Everyone did what was right in his own eyes**" (Judges 21:25b).

This is the moral climate of our modern world. Isaiah's description of Israel is no less true today as it was when it was first spoken: "**righteousness stands at a distance; truth has stumbled in the streets**" (Isaiah 59:14 NIV84).

What does the Bible say about race? How can we combat racism?

Today we talk about black people, white people, and people of color. And all the while I'm thinking, *Wait a minute! Are you seeing something I don't see?* I am technically classified as a Caucasian but when I look in the mirror I do not see the color white. What do we see when we look in the mirror? The answer is given to us by Ken Ham in an article where he wrote:

...all humans basically have the same skin color—a brown pigment called melanin. Although there are a couple of forms of

152 PASTOR, I HAVE A QUESTION

melanin and other pigments and factors playing minor roles in skin color, every human basically has a brown color.*

Wow! Imagine that! We're all just different shades of the *same* color.

What Race Are You?
You've probably filled out a form or two and noticed that the section where you have to indicate your race doesn't include "human" as an option. That makes more sense, right? Sure, there are various ethnicities, but regardless of their differences, all of us are still members of *one* human race.

Isn't that interesting? The two words that cause so much trouble in our culture — *color* and *race* — really aren't a problem since we're all members of the same race with different shades of the same skin color. And yet the world would have us believe that the best way to fight racism is to highlight and focus on those differences.

The only way to truly combat the issues of racism and ethnic inequality is to understand man's origin from the standpoint of God's Word. Acts 17:26 says, "From one man [God] made every nation of men, that they should inhabit the whole earth" (NIV84). That means no matter what shade of the same color we happen to wear on our skin, we are all created by God and are descendants of the same parentage. Focusing on that truth is what will truly set us free.

*Kevin Ham, "It's Not Just Black & White," *answersingeneris. org*, February 2008.

Is there a verse or passage I can use to convince people that a fetus is a human being?

Citing a specific verse can be challenging. There are many things in the Bible that are presumed to be true but are never really explained. Among them are:

- a Creator God who designed the universe

- the existence of right and wrong and mankind's natural ability to discern the difference between the two

- humans being created male and female

- the sacredness of God-given life

These things are known deep in the heart of man and remain true even though he desperately tries to silence the inner voice that confirms them. To look for a Bible verse to prove that a fetus is a human being is to leap-frog over the inward witness of man's conscience and attempt to prove something to him that he already knows full well but has simply denied. They will not be persuaded no matter how many convincing Scripture passages we quote because this issue is not a matter of knowledge but of choice.

And while they *do* acknowledge it as a matter of choice, their idea of what that "choice" means is that of a woman's right to decide for herself. But that's not the chief and utmost point. Ultimately, it's mankind's choosing to reject God and all He stands for. All the things we see today: abortion on demand, lawlessness, blatant sinful activity, rejection of marriage, rejection of gender, etc., – these are not the result of people not having enough information. They represent a wholesale rejection of God and as the Apostle Paul said, "**On**

account of these the wrath of God is coming" (Colossians 3:6).

The answer has always been the same: It starts with salvation through Jesus Christ and then the renewing of one's mind. We will not win people to our side before we win them to Christ. And they will not side with Christ until their minds have been renewed. There is no shortcut. There's no magical response that will turn the tide of public opinion. We must pray and ask the Lord of the Harvest to send more workers into the field.

Are women required to wear head coverings today?

This question comes up from time to time because of the Apostle Paul's remarks in 1 Corinthians 11 where he writes:

Every man who prays or prophesies with his head covered dishonors his head, but every wife who prays or prophesies with her head uncovered dishonors her head, since it is the same as if her head were shaven. For if a wife will not cover her head, then she should cut her hair short. But since it is disgraceful for a wife to cut off her hair or shave her head, let her cover her head. For a man ought not to cover his head, since he is the image and glory of God, but woman is the glory of man…That is why a wife ought to have a symbol of authority on her head, because of the angels. (vv. 4–7;10)

These comments are pretty strong, and the key to understanding them is found in **verse 10** where Paul reveals the purpose of a woman's head covering: "…**a wife ought to have**

a symbol of authority on her head..." You'll notice that Paul refers to a head covering as '**a symbol of authority**.' He is referring to the authority or headship of a man over his wife as established by God which, in Paul's day, was made crystal clear by a woman covering her head. This is still the case in some cultures, but in many places around the world it is no longer so. Women use other things to communicate their respect for God's order in marriage — which is the whole point of Paul's remarks.

In the Apostle Paul's culture, a woman's head covering carried a very strong message; but here in America, a woman with her head covered is unlikely to be viewed by others as someone expressing a biblical respect for her husband. In fact, when women are seen with some kind of "religious" head covering today, most Americans assume that it is simply a symbol of a religious affiliation and nothing more. The spirit of Paul's message to women was about showing respect and honor however that is best expressed.

Is wearing jewelry a sin?

One passage that is often brought up when discussing this topic is 1 Peter 3. It is used in many Christian circles to impose upon women the prohibition of wearing jewelry or anything else that might be considered "outward adornment" including makeup. But if you really look at this passage, you'll see that the subject of Peter's exhortation is *inward* or real beauty. He's challenging women to refuse to cave into whatever the world considers "beauty" (which is always external).

156 PASTOR, I HAVE A QUESTION

The passage goes like this:

Your beauty should not come from outward adornment, such as elaborate hairstyles and the wearing of gold jewelry or fine clothes. Rather, it should be that of your inner self, the unfading beauty of a gentle and quiet spirit, which is of great worth in God's sight. For this is the way the holy women of the past who put their hope in God used to adorn themselves... (1 Peter 3:3 – 5 NIV)

Rather than forbidding women to wear jewelry and fine clothes or preventing them from having elaborate hairstyles, Peter is simply saying, "Don't let those things become the definition of beauty." Instead, he encourages women to consider the example of Sarah, whose beauty came from within — characterized by a "gentle and quiet spirit."

There is always a tendency among some groups to read the New Testament with an Old Testament mindset. They read a passage like 1 Peter 3:3 – 5 and see nothing but prohibitions and rules. But what they neglect is the real focus of Peter's message which is meant to appeal to the heart, not to a dress code.

Another verse used to emphasize that women ought not to wear jewelry and such is Galatians 6:14 that says:

May I never boast except in the cross of our Lord Jesus Christ, through which the world has been crucified to me, and I to the world. (NIV)

The legalist assumes that this passage forbids the possession of anything that might cause boasting. Since some boast about their riches by displaying their fine jewelry, there are those who conclude that the use of such things is worldly and therefore must be forsaken. But what if a woman owned and even wore fine jewelry, but in her heart cared nothing for it because jewelry for her was *never* a reason to boast? Would such a person still be forbidden from having and wearing jewelry?

The legalist is forced to say yes for an answer. And that's what's wrong with legalistic rules — they almost never take into consideration the condition of the heart. Instead, they make general rules that everyone must conform to or else be shunned. But they forget that it's possible to never wear jewelry or makeup or fine clothing and *still* have a heart that is boastful and proud.

That's why God communicates to us repeatedly throughout the Scriptures that He is primarily concerned with our hearts — not our external appearance. Man is concerned with the exterior, but God looks at the heart (see 1 Samuel 16:7).

Does the Bible tell us to confess our sins to everyone?

People who ask this question usually cite passages such as: John 3:16-22; 1 John 1:7-10; Ephesians 5:11-13; and James 5:16. Let's tackle the first three on the list.

John 3:16-22; 1 John 1:7-10; and Ephesians 5:11-13 all speak of coming into and walking in the light. People often interpret these references to mean "coming clean" or confessing one's sins. But those passages really speak of agreeing with God about our sinful condition. In fact, the word *confess* literally means "to agree." God has declared all mankind to be sinful, and it is by personally confessing our

158   PASTOR, I HAVE A QUESTION

sin that we are essentially agreeing with Him. The person who does so is said to come into the light and walk in the light.

Furthermore, these passages speak of "confessing our sins *to* God." There's nothing here about spilling our guts about your past mistakes to everyone we know.

Now let's look at the last passage. On the surface, James 5:16 seems to be telling us to confess our sins "to one another."

Therefore, confess your sins to one another and pray for one another, that you may be healed. The prayer of a righteous person has great power as it is working.

But if you read the verses surrounding that text, you'll discover that James was addressing the subject of healing for those suffering physical infirmities.

Is anyone among you sick? (James 5:14)

His recommendation is that believers should call for the elders of the local church and have them pray the prayer of faith over the sick person and anoint them with oil. We can then infer that it is within the context of physical healing that he goes on to speak of confessing sin. The *point* of confessing sins to one another isn't just to get something off our shoulders — it's to encourage the healing process.

This is one of those passages where we need to apply wisdom and caution. Confessing our sins *to just anyone* is reckless and dangerous. Why? Because there are some in the Body of Christ who simply aren't ready for that kind of information.

When I was fairly new in the Lord, someone came to me — in what I believe was a sincere desire to be honest and transparent — and confessed to having very negative feelings toward me. That person recognized that it was wrong to feel that way and apologized, but I have to tell you, I was left with a very bad feeling. My faith wasn't strong and I allowed such honest confession to really haunt me for quite some time. Before that conversation I was completely oblivious to that person's feelings, but after finding out the truth, I allowed that knowledge to ruin any chance for a healthy relationship.

In his letter to the Romans, as well as in his first letter to the Corinthians, Paul spoke often of the brother whose faith is weak, and how mature believers have a responsibility not to injure that person or create an occasion for stumbling. There are other passages that specifically tell us to be mindful, seeing to it that our speech toward others is always edifying.

Let no corrupting talk come out of your mouths, but only such as is good for building up, as fits the occasion, that it may give grace to those who hear. (Ephesians 4:29)

...we urge you, brothers, admonish the idle, encourage the fainthearted, help the weak, be patient with them all. (1 Thessalonians 5:14)

So, to whom should you confess your sins?

I believe wisdom would tell you to only confess your sins to those who are mature in their faith and can pray with and for you. Pastors, elders, and ministry leaders are a good bet, especially if you know them to be faithful in their walk with Christ and full of wisdom and discretion.

Remember, opening up to just anyone about your sinful past could be a recipe for disaster. But if you feel you're being directed by the Lord to confess your sins in the presence of another believer, ask the Lord who He would have you connect with, and make sure the Lord is opening the door before you walk through it.

One last thought: We all have skeletons in our closet in the sense that we've done things in the past we're not proud of. But do I feel compelled to confess all my past sins? Heavens, no! It would be neither helpful nor encouraging to do so. My Bible tells me that I am a "new creation" in Christ Jesus. The old me is gone, the new has come (2 Corinthians 5:17). I have confessed my sins to God and I am completely confident that His forgiveness is mine by virtue of the cross. That's not to say I've never confessed my sins to a brother in Christ, because on occasion I have. But whenever I do, I know that the brother I'm speaking to can handle my confession and will stand with me in prayer for healing and restoration.

Am I rejecting God by going to the doctor and taking medicine?

How we view our physical bodies and the care we give them is unprecedented in human history. There's never been a time when people welcomed sickness and death but, reading the Bible, it becomes clear that our modern ideas about living disease and pain-free are rather new and radical from the attitudes of people in days gone by. Today we are virtually obsessed with health-related concerns and sustaining what we call the "quality of life." Every news program contains a health segment, and electronic devices that claim to monitor health are selling like hotcakes. With health-related talk at a fever pitch, I am genuinely concerned about our unrestrained focus.

WHAT DOES THE BIBLE SAY ABOUT... 161

Only God knows where faith begins and ends and where doubt takes over. One man may consult a doctor and yet maintain complete trust in the Lord, while another man may never darken the door of a clinic but still have *zero* faith in God's ability to heal. It's very tough to judge another person's heart and God has made it clear to me on many occasions that I'm not qualified to do so.

I go to doctors and take medicine when needed, but my hope is *not* in those things. I believe God has total control over the day of my death, and almost daily I offer Him lordship over my aging body since it belongs to Him in the first place (see 1 Corinthians 6:19–20). Even when I take a pill I do so with prayer saying: *"Lord, this pill was prescribed by a human doctor who is fallible and prone to mistakes. Only You are perfect and truly know what's going on in my life and body. So I put my faith in You and I trust You to cause this pill to do what it's supposed to do. Amen!"*

I don't believe that using modern medicine needs to be a breach of faith. It could be for some — but once again, I can't be the judge of that. There's an example in the Bible of someone who did place all his hope in doctors. You can read about King Asa in 2 Chronicles 16. He started out as a good king, but toward the end of his life this is what was written about him:

In the thirty-ninth year of his reign [King] Asa was afflicted with a disease in his feet. Though his disease was severe, even in his illness he did not seek help from the Lord, but only from the physicians. (v.12 NIV84)

Notice that God's Word doesn't chastise Asa for consulting doctors, but rather for not seeking the Lord's help. His error was placing all his hope in man — something God absolutely does not want us to do.

Stop trusting in man, who has but a breath in his nostrils. Of what account is he? (Isaiah 2:22 NIV84)

But here's the crazy part: Even though God tells us not to trust in man, He doesn't forbid us from using man. Even God uses men to get things done. When the nation of Israel went into the Promised Land under Joshua and began to fight against the Canaanite nations, God used the men in the Israelite army to do the fighting, while at the same time telling them not to trust in their own ability to win their battles but rather to trust in Him.

So think about it: Why did God have those soldiers get ready for battle? He told them repeatedly that the battle belonged to the Lord — does that mean then that the soldiers' act of strapping on their swords is equivalent to rejecting God? Why did they even bother to grab their shields and bring their bows and arrows? Wasn't the act of bringing those weapons to the battle a breach of faith? No, it wasn't. Why? Because God chose to use those men to get His will accomplished.

In the same way, God can and does use doctors to carry out His will. Does He have to use them? Of course not! God can fulfill His will without using medical professionals, just like He didn't have to use the army of Israel. But instead, He chose to work His will through them. I believe God can choose to work His will through doctors and medicine too. He's not limited by anything.

Is getting a vaccine an act of unbelief?

NOTE: This question is not about the COVID-19 vaccine. Pastor Paul is responding to a general question about vaccines, medicines, and doctors, and how such things fit into a life of faith.

What might be an act of unbelief for one person isn't necessarily an act of unbelief for another. It all comes down to the heart. A man may submit to a surgical procedure but place himself completely in the hands of God for the outcome, while another may undergo the same procedure and place his complete trust in doctors and medicines for the desired outcome. It depends on the individual and where their ultimate trust and confidence lie.

The Bible doesn't specifically address vaccines or even say much about doctors for that matter. But it does talk a lot about trusting God. I suppose all those passages about trusting God with all our heart explain why some people claim that seeking medical help by going to the doctor and taking medicine is not walking by faith. But those very same people walk into grocery and clothing stores every day and think nothing of it even though Jesus promised that God would feed and clothe us (see Matthew 6:25 – 33). Wouldn't that also be considered a faithless act in light of God's promise?

Real faith is a matter of the heart. One may get a vaccine and remain fully convinced that God is in charge of his life and health, while another may expresses this same faith by rejecting the vaccine. Each one should be fully convinced in their own heart and not cast judgment upon the other.

Does the Bible forbid Christian business owners from providing services to homosexuals?

The Bible does *not* direct Christian business owners to refuse service to homosexuals. I've taught through the entire Bible multiple times and I can tell you there is no passage in Scripture that specifically commands that type of action. It means that whether a Christian business owner denies service to homosexuals becomes a matter of conscience.

The Bible makes it very clear that homosexuality is contrary to God's intention for marriage. That much is plain. But the fact that homosexuality is considered sinful in the Bible should not be a reason for us Christians to refuse to interact with those who practice that sin. (Besides, if we do that, who's going to be around to share the love of Christ?) In fact, the Apostle Paul says otherwise. Check out this passage:

I have written you in my letter not to associate with sexually immoral people—not at all meaning the people of this world who are immoral, or the greedy and swindlers, or idolaters. In that case you would have to leave this world. (1 Corinthians 5:9–10 NIV 84)

Apparently, some of the Christians in Corinth believed that they should withdraw from any association with anyone who practiced an openly unbiblical lifestyle. But Paul reminded them that to dissociate or break away from those people wasn't even possible!

Over the past few years there have been Christian bakers that made headlines for choosing not to provide their services to same-sex couples. I think what most people don't understand is *why* a Christian-owned bakery would refuse to accommodate a homosexual wedding. People often say, "Hey, they're in business to provide a service." But the truth is, some bakeries do *not* consider themselves to be merely providing a service. They would tell you that they are actually taking part in the ceremony and celebration of the marriage — much like a pastor being asked to officiate, or a musician being asked to provide music. For many, it is so much more than rendering a service. It's also sharing a part of their lives. That's why there are Christian business owners who feel that their conscience will not allow them to participate.

That said, it remains a matter of conscience. I believe decisions based on conscience should be respected, regardless of which side of this fence you find yourself on.

Is Christmas a holiday with pagan roots?

Let me begin by responding to the premise that Christmas is a pagan celebration. Imagine for a moment that you, a believer and follower of Jesus, live right next door to someone who is a pagan. (By the way, a pagan is someone who believes in many gods.) Now imagine that on a particular day of the year, both you and your neighbor choose to celebrate something related to your faith. Your neighbor, as a pagan, celebrates his pagan deities and holds a feast and invites his friends. You, on the other hand, use that very same day to celebrate the Lord God who sent His Son to save you from your sin. Like your neighbor, you also hold a feast and invite your friends.

Now, are you celebrating a pagan holiday simply because your celebration lands on the same day as your neighbor's?

If pagans at one time in history used December 25 to cele-

166 PASTOR, I HAVE A QUESTION

brate their pagan deities, are we then to consider the date forever off-limits to believers of the one true God? The God whom you and I serve created *all* things — including the days of the year. And if that's the case, then no day of the year should be off-limits to Christians.

I have been celebrating Christmas ever since I can remember. For me, December 25 has *always* been about celebrating the incarnation — God becoming a man in the Person of Jesus Christ. When I grew up I learned that December 25 had also been used for pagan celebrations. But that information didn't really affect me at all because paganism has never been part of my life. For me, December 25 has only ever been a celebration of God's goodness and mercy. And it remains so to this day.

Here's the point: To celebrate a pagan holiday I must: (1) be a pagan and (2) worship what pagans worship. But these descriptions don't apply to me. I am a child of the Living God and I serve and worship Him alone. All 365 days of the year belong to Him who made them and what that means for me is that I do not have to surrender one single day of the calendar to pagans who are in no position to take the days my God created as if those days were their own.

Someone might say, "Hang on, pastor! The Bible strictly forbids having and decorating Christmas trees. It's right there in the Bible in the book of Jeremiah!"

But does the Bible really forbid that? Let's look closely:

Hear what the LORD says to you, O house of Israel. This is what the LORD says: "Do not learn the ways of the nations or be terrified by signs in the sky, though the nations are terrified by them. For the customs of the peoples are worthless; they cut a tree out of the forest, and a craftsman shapes it with his chisel.

They adorn it with silver and gold; they fasten it with hammer and nails so it will not totter." (Jeremiah 10:1–4 NIV84)

Looking closely, we find that the passage is *not* talking about Christmas trees. God is talking to the nation of Israel about their pagan neighbors and how they carved idols out of wood and covered them (literally coated them) with gold and silver and worshiped them. Did you catch the part about the craftsman cutting a tree and shaping it with his chisel? That pertains to the idol being shaped into the form of their pagan deities. Jeremiah was describing carved pagan idols that people bowed down to and worshiped. None of these things apply to Christmas trees and Christians certainly don't worship them.

It's important for believers to understand the context of biblical passages and learn to rightly handle the Word of truth. If you are conscientiously opposed to having a Christmas tree in your home, that's your personal business and is ultimately between you and the Lord. But if someone tells you they're celebrating the birth of Jesus Christ, it's best to give them the benefit of the doubt and refrain from judging them based on the way they hold or carry out that celebration.

168   PASTOR, I HAVE A QUESTION

What does God say about a believer taking a life, e.g., capital punishment or killing in defense?

When it comes to taking a life, the Bible *does* make a distinction between murder, which is the taking of a life for vengeance or some other indiscriminate reason; and the taking of a life for the purpose of punishment or military action, which assumes a defensive act.

Within the context of Israel's theocratic rule established in the Mosaic Law, God explicitly outlined a system of capital punishment for certain crimes. This practice was certainly active prior to the Mosaic Law and is still enforced in many lands to this day.

Capital punishment is actually founded on the principle that all life is sacred. The idea behind it is that the decision to take a life is never made by the ones who were hurt by the crime, i.e., the family and loved ones the victim left behind; but rather by those whose responsibility it is to impartially determine the motive and severity of the offense and deliver an appropriate and justified response, i.e., the judge presiding over the trial (in some states). I'm fully aware that some people believe that taking a life for a crime is *never* justified and I respect that opinion, but it simply isn't supported biblically.

Part of the confusion in this matter stems from the way the King James Version of the Bible renders Exodus 20:13 which says, "Thou shalt not kill." At face value this verse seems to place a divine prohibition on the taking of any life for any reason. However, the more modern translations clear up the confusion by correctly rendering this verse: "***You shall not murder.***"

The Hebrew word for murder refers specifically to that which is premeditated and carries the connotation of human death caused by carelessness or neglect. From here we can conclude that death brought as the result of justice or military action is not in view in the abovementioned verse.

In Romans 13 the Apostle Paul spoke of the right of governmental authorities to dispense justice, saying:

Let every person be subject to the governing authorities. For there is no authority except from God, and those that exist have been instituted by God. Therefore whoever resists the authorities resists what God has appointed, and those who resist will incur judgment. For rulers are not a terror to good conduct, but to bad. Would you have no fear of the one who is in authority? Then do what is good, and you will receive his approval, for he is God's servant for your good. But if you do wrong, be afraid, for he does not bear the sword in vain. For he is the servant of God, an avenger who carries out God's wrath on the wrongdoer. (v.1–4)

This is admittedly a challenging topic, add to that the fact that many people are very passionate in their opposition to the taking of life for *any* reason, including justice or military action. However, the God who created the universe and those who inhabit it determined a system of justice that included the taking of life in certain situations. Far from marginalizing the sacredness of life, this idea serves to underscore and affirm that life is precious and should be protected.

Can Christians be involved in political affairs?

It's true we're told in the Word to focus our minds on "things that are above" (Colossians 3:1–2). We're also told that our "citizenship is in heaven" (Philippians 3:20). I guess someone could use these passages to make the point that political involvement is unwarranted for believers. But the Apostle Paul also urged us to pray for the leaders of our government (see 1 Timothy 2:1–2). This command shows that God wants our presence in this world to make a difference.

"Wait a minute!" someone might say. "Praying for our nation's leaders is one thing. But voting and running for office is quite another! We're never told to participate that way!" And that's true. But remember, the kind of political involvement you and I are privileged to have here in America was virtually unknown in biblical times. Democracy as we know it was unheard of, and a political process that involved citizens casting a vote was incredibly rare in the ancient world. No wonder the Apostle Paul never spoke of it. Even when citizens *were* allowed to vote in ancient Roman elections, often the outcome was determined by the upper class or by those in power who had already pre-selected their candidate of choice. The privilege to cast our vote along with our ability to change the political landscape is truly unique.

I believe it's possible to take advantage of our political freedom to cast our vote and *still* keep our minds focused on things above. It's true, we are citizens of heaven, but we are also citizens of the country in which we live. And as those who are commissioned to be salt and light in this world, I believe we have a responsibility to positively impact the way our country operates. In fact, throughout the centuries it was believers in Jesus who spearheaded change in areas like the slave trade both here and in Europe. They did it by influencing the political process and changing the laws of the land.

Participating in the political process does *not* mean we've sold out to the world or that we're trusting in man. Biblical Christians fully understand that the heart of mankind is corrupt and deceitful. Furthermore, we know that the condition of this world will go from bad to worse (see 2 Timothy 3:1–5). But until the Lord calls us home, we ought to be using whatever opportunities and freedoms the Lord has granted us to bring the light of His presence into this dark world.

Is civil disobedience biblical? What about government overthrow? Can the American Revolution be considered a type of government overthrow?

Yes, we are told to obey the established laws of the land in which we live. And yes, there are biblical precedents for what we call "civil disobedience" for any time the government may establish a law or ordinance that would seek to render ineffective our obedience to God's Word.

For example, if our nation ever went so far as to declare that evangelizing was illegal, those of us who take God's Word seriously would have to say: "**Whether it is right in the sight of God to listen to you rather than to God, you must judge, for we cannot but speak of what we have seen and heard**" (Acts 4:19–20). And we would say this because we have already received an explicit directive from our Lord to go into all the world and "**make disciples of all nations**" (Matthew 28:19). That command trumps any contradictory edict or law of man that might compel us to obey.

As far as "overthrowing the government" goes, I'm not sure the American Revolution entirely qualifies as a genuine government overthrow. It's true that the American colonists were attempting to gain their independence from British rule here in America, but as far as I know, they never took their battle to Britain in any attempt to unseat the Monarchy or overthrow the government there. They seemed content to let England function with whatever authority they saw fit. They simply wanted the British to leave them alone so they could live in the Americas with a new Constitution and new freedoms. It seems like what we're really asking is whether there *are* biblical grounds for a political separatist movement when we feel our rights and religious freedoms are being violated.

I would not be comfortable with anyone using God's Word to justify or substantiate any type of government overthrow. Much of the New Testament was written during times of oppressive and dictatorial leaders and governing bodies, and still the apostles and writers of the New Testament refrained from using any language that would encourage believers to put their energy toward any kind of government coup or illegal government reform. In fact, we are reminded in God's Word that our true citizenship is in heaven (Philippians 3:20). As to participating in something like the American Revolution, I believe it would be up to the conscience of every individual before God. Looking back, I would have to say I'm glad those early Americans did what they did.

Chapter 11

OLD TESTAMENT AND THE LAW OF MOSES

- Where did Old Testament believers go when they died? 175

- Are the Jews still God's chosen people? 177

- What about keeping the Sabbath? Are Christians under the Law of Moses? 179

- When did the Sabbath change from Saturday to Sunday? 185

- Can Christians claim the promises that were made to Israel in the Old Testament? 186

- Where did Cain get his wife? 187

- Why do some Christians reject a literal interpretation of Genesis and the Creation account? 188

174   PASTOR, I HAVE A QUESTION

- Do the dietary laws in Leviticus still apply to believers today? 190

- Why were concubines allowed in Old Testament times? 191

- Why did people live so long in the Old Testament? 192

- Why was the Day of Atonement necessary for Israel if sacrifices were being made daily? 194

Where did Old Testament believers go when they died?

It is often assumed that under the new covenant we are saved by accepting Jesus as our Savior and that believers under the old covenant were saved by their obedience to the Law of Moses. But that is not at all true. The argument of the Apostle Paul throughout Romans is that the law was never meant as a means to save anyone, and he makes it abundantly clear that "**no one will be declared righteous in God's sight by the works of the law**" (Romans 3:20 NIV).

So if people weren't saved by keeping the Law in Old Testament times, how then were they saved? The simple answer is the same way we are saved today — BY FAITH. The Old Testament sacrificial system merely gave the Israelites a graphic touchpoint for placing their faith in God's goodness and mercy. It provided a clear example of a blood sacrifice involving the exchange of one life for another — all pointing beautifully to the final sacrifice of Jesus Christ which was yet to come.

People in Old Testament times died placing their faith in things hoped for and things not yet seen. As to where they went after death, Jesus made it clear that prior to His death on the cross which opened the way to heaven, no one who had died before that time had ever gone into heaven.

No one has ascended into heaven except he who descended from heaven, the Son of Man. (John 3:13)

So if they didn't end up in heaven, where did they go? Jesus revealed the answer to this question in a story he told which is recounted in Luke's Gospel account. As you read the verses below, take special note of the descriptions given about the place where people went after death.

176   PASTOR, I HAVE A QUESTION

"There was a rich man who was clothed in purple and fine linen and who feasted sumptuously every day. And at his gate was laid a poor man named Lazarus, covered with sores, who desired to be fed with what fell from the rich man's table. Moreover, even the dogs came and licked his sores. The poor man died and was carried by the angels to Abraham's side. The rich man also died and was buried, and in Hades, being in torment, he lifted up his eyes and saw Abraham far off and Lazarus at his side. And he called out, 'Father Abraham, have mercy on me, and send Lazarus to dip the end of his finger in water and cool my tongue, for I am in anguish in this flame.' But Abraham said, 'Child, remember that you in your lifetime received your good things, and Lazarus in like manner bad things; but now he is comforted here, and you are in anguish. And besides all this, between us and you a great chasm has been fixed, in order that those who would pass from here to you may not be able, and none may cross from there to us.' And he said, 'Then I beg you, father, to send him to my father's house—for I have five brothers—so that he may warn them, lest they also come into this place of torment.' But Abraham said, 'They have Moses and the Prophets; let them hear them.' And he said, 'No, father Abraham, but if someone goes to them from the dead, they will repent.' He said to him, 'If they do not hear Moses and the Prophets, neither will they be convinced if someone should rise from the dead.'" (Luke 16:19–31)

It's important to note that this story is *not* a parable. This is a true account concerning real people and real places. *(Notice Jesus' usage of a proper name in these verses — something that was never done when merely relating a parable.)*

When Lazarus (no relation to the man of the same name whom Jesus raised from the dead) died, he was taken to a place which Jesus referred to as "Abraham's side" (the Greek word is literally translated *bosom*.) This is certainly not heaven, but a kind of holding place of comfort where those who died in faith awaited entrance into heaven.

The rich man in the story also died and Jesus said that he was sent to a "place of torment" called Hades (which literally means *the grave* or *hell*). The incredible thing is that these places were in proximity and it was possible for the inhabitants of each place to converse, although moving from one place to the other was impossible.

I believe this story gives us a unique glimpse into the place where those who died prior to the cross of Christ awaited the opening of heaven. Now that Jesus has paid the full price for our sin, all who have placed their faith in His finished work on the cross are immediately ushered into the presence of God upon death. The words that Jesus spoke to the penitent thief on the cross are now the very words we can all confidently embrace: "Truly, I say to you, today you will be with me in Paradise" (Luke 23:43).

Are the Jews still God's chosen people?

The Bible tells us that God first chose Abraham and made him many wonderful promises, one of which was the promise that through him all nations would be blessed (see Galatians 3:8). These promises of God to Abraham were then repeated to his son Isaac and later to his grandson Jacob, who was renamed Israel.

When we speak of Israel as God's chosen people, we're really saying that God chose Abraham and his descendants after him through his son Isaac. So, why doesn't it seem as if Israel is a favored nation today?

178   PASTOR, I HAVE A QUESTION

At this time in history God is working through the Church which pertains to the Body of Christ — the people who belong to Jesus and are also referred to in the Bible as God's "chosen" (1 Peter 2:9). However, that doesn't mean God has abandoned Israel. Far from it.

No other nation in the world was set apart for God in the same way as Israel, and God still has plans for them in the future. In fact, much of what the Bible has to say prophetically about Israel remains to be fulfilled. And when Jesus returns physically to this earth, He will return to Israel.

But God's timetable for Israel has been put on hold during what we call the "Church Age." Once the Church is removed or "caught up...in the clouds to meet the Lord in the air," (1 Thessalonians 4:17) God will once again set in motion His plan for Israel and its people.

Although both Israel and the Church are referred to in the Scriptures as "chosen," there are significant differences between the two. Israel possesses a physical kingdom, while the Church possesses a spiritual kingdom. The promises God made to Israel in the Law of Moses are physical blessings, but the promises made to the Church through Jesus Christ are spiritual in nature (see Ephesians 1:3). Israel is not the Church and the Church is not Israel, yet both have a very special place in God's plan of redemption.

What about keeping the Sabbath? Are Christians under the Law of Moses?

I would like to get started by stating the following points which I will then explain below:

Truth Statement 1. God made a covenant with Israel that included Sabbath-keeping. That covenant is called the "Mosaic Covenant" and it was limited to God and Israel. The Mosaic Covenant was *not* made with the Church.

Truth Statement 2. The meaning of the Sabbath was fulfilled in the Person and work of Jesus Christ.

Regarding the first truth statement: There is an assumption by many Christians that the covenant God made with Israel is fully binding on the New Testament Church — the Body of Christ. I say this is an "assumption" because it is *not* supported in the Word of God. The Scripture is clear that God established the Mosaic Covenant between Himself and Israel. Consider the following passage:

Therefore the people of Israel shall keep the Sabbath, observing the Sabbath throughout their generations, as a covenant forever. (Exodus 31:16)

This passage tells us that: (1) Israel is to keep the Sabbath and that (2) the Sabbath is part of a lasting covenant. Again, that covenant is between God and Israel.

Is there biblical evidence that God has made a *new* covenant with the Church? Yes! (By the way, this New Covenant was *first* offered to Israel and the Gentiles were to be included later.) This was prophesied in Jeremiah 31 and goes like this:

"The time is coming," declares the LORD, "when <u>I will make a new covenant</u> with the house of Israel and with the house of Judah. <u>It</u>

180 PASTOR, I HAVE A QUESTION

will not be like the covenant I made with their forefathers when I took them by the hand to lead them out of Egypt, because they broke my covenant, though I was a husband to them," declares the LORD. "This is the covenant I will make with the house of Israel after that time," declares the LORD. "I will put my law in their minds and write it on their hearts. I will be their God, and they will be my people. No longer will a man teach his neighbor, or a man his brother, saying, 'Know the LORD,' because they will all know me, from the least of them to the greatest," declares the LORD. "For I will forgive their wickedness and will remember their sins no more." (vv. 31–34 NIV84)

There are four important things to note from this passage. Each point has a corresponding text from the Scripture which I have underlined above:

1. God promised a time when He would make a new covenant with His people.

2. He said it would not be like the old covenant made through Moses.

3. A key to this new covenant is that He would take His Law and write it on His people's hearts. (A very lovely reference to the indwelling of the Holy Spirit, which did NOT happen under the old covenant.)

4. The new covenant would be a covenant offering forgiveness.

I want to emphasize point # 2 here: God specifically spoke through Jeremiah saying the New Covenant would *not* be like the Old Covenant.

Now, let's ask the question: When was this New Covenant brought into play for God's people?

OLD TESTAMENT AND THE LAW OF MOSES   181

The New Covenant was inaugurated through the death and resurrection of Jesus. At the Last Supper, Jesus took the cup and said, "**This cup is the new covenant in my blood, which is poured out for you**" (Luke 22:20 NIV).

Christians are under the New Covenant established by Jesus through His death on the cross. It is a "new covenant in [His] blood."

In his letter to the Romans the Apostle Paul writes:

For sin shall no longer be your master, because you are not under the law, but under grace. What then? Shall we sin because we are not under the law but under grace? By no means! (Romans 6:14–15 NIV)

Twice in those two verses Paul declared that believers are "not under the law." That means we are not bound to the Law as a means of being accepted by God. We are accepted *by faith*, because without faith it is "impossible to please God" (Hebrews 11:6) and because the righteous "shall live by faith" (Habakkuk 2:4).

Okay, let's look at the second truth statement I made at the very beginning: **The meaning of the Sabbath was fulfilled in the Person and work of Jesus Christ.**

Do you remember what Jesus said about the Law? He said:

"Do not think that I have come to abolish the Law or the Prophets; I have not come to abolish them but to fulfill them." (Matthew 5:17)

Jesus claimed that His coming was to "fulfill the Law." Let's look at how He fulfilled the Sabbath.

182 PASTOR, I HAVE A QUESTION

Sabbath-keeping was all about *resting.* God commanded the nation of Israel to *rest* on the Sabbath, which meant to do no regular work. But the Jews took that simple command and they made it ridiculously complex and horribly legalistic. When Jesus healed a man on the Sabbath the Jewish leaders were outraged and wanted to kill Jesus because of it — that's how far they had fallen away from God's original intent for the Sabbath. Jesus had to remind them, "**The Sabbath was made for man, not man for the Sabbath**" (Mark 2:27).

The Sabbath was made *for man to rest.* In the New Testament book of Hebrews, the idea of entering God's rest takes a prominent place in chapter four where the author of Hebrews makes this incredible statement:

For we who have believed enter that rest... (Hebrews 4:3)

He goes on to explain his statement a few verses later:

...there remains a Sabbath rest for the people of God, for whoever has entered God's rest has also <u>rested from his works</u> as God did from his. Let us therefore strive to enter that rest, so that no one may fall by the same sort of disobedience. (vv. 9–11)

Notice the words I've underlined above. The writer of Hebrews tells us that those who have "rested from his works" have, in fact, entered into God's rest. We see from the context of Hebrews that the author is speaking of the work of Jesus on the cross. What does that have to do with rest? Those who *believe* and trust that the work of Jesus on the cross is *enough* have entered into God's rest. Why? Because they are **resting** in the finished work of Jesus.

This resting is powerfully foretold in the substance of the Passover celebration. When God was delivering Israel from their bondage to slavery in Egypt, He had Moses instruct the people of Israel to slaughter a young lamb and to mark the

OLD TESTAMENT AND THE LAW OF MOSES   183

doorposts of their homes with its blood. They were told that during the night the Lord would "**pass through Egypt and strike down every firstborn of both people and animals**." But as for the Israelites, "**the blood will be a sign for you on the houses where you are, and when I see the blood, I will pass over you**" Exodus 12:12–13 (NIV).

The people of Israel were literally sheltering under the blood of the lamb. They were "resting" in God's solution for their deliverance. There was nothing they could do except to *trust* that God's Word was true and that the blood of the lamb would be sufficient.

This presents for us a New Testament picture of Sabbath-keeping. Rather than keeping a single day of the week, we are resting in the finished work of Jesus on the cross seven days a week. And in doing so, by faith, we are "keeping" the Sabbath. As the writer of Hebrews said, "**For we who have believed enter that rest**" (Hebrews 4:3).

This is why the New Testament writers never told believers to "keep" the Sabbath in the Old Covenant way. (Remember, the New Covenant would *not* be like the old one.) Not once are believers in the New Testament told to keep a specific day. In fact, the opposite is true.

One man considers one day more sacred than another; another man considers every day alike. Each one should be fully convinced in his own mind. He who regards one day as special, does so to the Lord. He who eats meat, eats to the Lord, for he gives thanks to God; and he who abstains, does so to the Lord and gives thanks to God. (Romans 14:5–6 NIV84)

If Sabbath-keeping was in fact required for us to reach heaven, why in the world would the Apostle Paul say what he did in those verses from Romans 14? Also, check out the

184   PASTOR, I HAVE A QUESTION

following passage:

Therefore do not let anyone judge you by what you eat or drink, or with regard to a religious festival, a New Moon celebration or a Sabbath day. These are a shadow of the things that were to come; the reality, however, is found in Christ. (Colossians 2:16–17 NIV)

Here Paul clearly says that Sabbath-keeping (as it was done under the Old Covenant) is a "**shadow of the things that were to come.**" He tells us that the reality of the Sabbath is found in Christ. He is the fulfillment of the Sabbath regulations through His death on the cross. When we rest in what He did for us, we keep the Sabbath.

Finally, look at Paul's words in Romans:

Do we then overthrow the law by this faith? By no means! On the contrary, we uphold the law. (Romans 3:31)

Faith *upholds* the Law because our faith is in Jesus — who fulfilled the Law for us in every way. The law was never intended as a means of salvation. God *never* promised that by keeping the Law people would obtain heaven. Salvation is offered one way: through faith in Jesus Christ and His finished work on the cross.

When did the Sabbath change from Saturday to Sunday?

Never! The biblical Sabbath was established as part of the Mosaic Covenant between God and Israel and has *always* been Saturday, the seventh day of the week.

The obvious follow-up question to this would be: *Why then do Christians observe Sunday instead of Saturday as a special day of worship?*

Christians *gather* on Sunday, but they do not *observe* it as a special day in the same way the Jews were commanded to observe the Sabbath. Early believers gathered on Sunday simply because it was "the Lord's day"– the day Jesus was raised from the tomb. But nowhere in the Bible are Christians called to observe or keep that day or any other day for that matter.

This doesn't mean the early believers didn't come under fire about this. Some in Colossae were being criticized for not keeping the seventh-day Sabbath, so the Apostle Paul wrote to them saying:

Therefore do not let anyone judge you by what you eat or drink, or with regard to a religious festival, a New Moon celebration or a Sabbath day. These are a shadow of the things that were to come; the reality, however, is found in Christ. (Colossians 2:16–17 NIV84)

The Christians in the region of Galatia were bowing to pressure to observe special days, which prompted the Apostle's following comments, "**You are observing special days and months and seasons and years! I fear for you, that somehow I have wasted my efforts on you**" (Galatians 4:10–11 NIV84).

186   PASTOR, I HAVE A QUESTION

Why did Paul make these comments about the Sabbath? It's because Sabbath regulations were established between God and Israel. Those regulations do not extend to the Church, which is under a completely different covenant (see Romans 6:14–15; Exodus 31:13–17).

Can Christians claim the promises that were made to Israel in the Old Testament?

Some of them we can, and others we cannot. Many of the promises given to the Israelites are simply promises based on God's care for His children and speak of His own faithfulness and goodness. Those statements and promises are for all time.

That said, we need to understand that there are many promises in the Old Testament that were conditioned upon Israel's obedience to the commands of the Mosaic Covenant. Those we cannot claim because they were given to Israel and pertained to the land that was promised to Abraham as well as the blessing that would attend their obedience to the Law. Those blessings included victory over enemies, fruitfulness both physically and agriculturally, and even long life.

The important question here is: Do these promises apply to Christians today? The answer is *no*, and here's why:

1. The Church does not — as some have wrongfully taught — take the place of Israel.

2. We, the Body of Christ, do not function under the terms of the Mosaic Covenant.

There is far too great a tendency for Christians to assume that everything we read is for our personal application. The Apostle Paul tells us that we are "not under law" (Romans 6:14) which means we are not involved in the covenant that God made with Israel through Moses.

Ours is a covenant of grace, the terms of which were fulfilled by Christ. The promises made to us are entirely different from those extended to Israel. Rather than a physical kingdom with physical blessings, the Church has been offered "better promises" according to Hebrews 8:6. These include a spiritual kingdom with spiritual blessings (see Ephesians 1:3).

Where did Cain get his wife?

This question gets asked quite a lot because when reading through Genesis we come to chapter four where Cain is punished by God for murdering his brother and immediately afterward we're told that "**Cain knew his wife**" (v.17). People quite naturally want to know where this woman came from since she seemed to have popped up out of nowhere.

A lot of people who ask this question don't take into consideration the fact that Bible writers often disregarded anyone who didn't make a contribution to the current narrative. In other words, we read about Cain, Abel, and Seth because of their key contributions to the storyline. But that doesn't mean they were the only children born to Adam and Eve. Not by a long shot.

Cain and Abel are introduced to us in the opening verses of Genesis 4, but in verse 3 there's an important phrase that says, "**In the course of time Cain brought to the Lord an offering**..." The phrase "In the course of time" presents to us the passing of a considerable amount of time during which the world's population obviously grew very rapidly. How did it grow? Genesis 5:4 tells us that Adam lived another 800 years after the birth of Seth, "**and he had other sons and daughters**." Adam and Eve therefore had many more children who grew up and had children of their own, who also grew up and had children.

The Bible doesn't record how long Cain lived, but if his lifespan was anywhere near that of his brother Seth it would have been in excess of 900 years. In just a fraction of that time the population growth would have been sufficient for Cain to have had several choices for a wife. And even though the woman he married had been a close relative, the purity of the gene pool in those early days of human history allowed for healthy children.

Why do some Christians reject a literal interpretation of Genesis and the Creation account?

Evolutionary thinking has greatly influenced how people view the literal Creation account as recorded in the Bible. In most cases, people have become convinced that the earth is millions, or even billions of years old, and this has resulted in the need to reject a literal interpretation of Genesis 1–11.

Taking those verses allegorically comes with dangers and pitfalls, and one of them is the likelihood of *twisting* or *corrupting* the essential message of the Gospel. An example of a foundational truth that is vulnerable to being shaken due to the allegorizing of the first 11 chapters of Genesis is the Apostle Paul's statement about the origin of death:

Therefore, just as sin entered the world through one man, and death through sin, and in this way death came to all men, because all sinned... (Romans 5:12 NIV84)

Those who reject a literal interpretation of Genesis and the Creation account are forced to believe that death did *not* enter the world through one man, as Paul wrote. Instead, they believe that death was part of God's original creative design since they are forced to believe animals were living and dying millions of years before man came upon the scene. They must *reject* Paul's statement and all that goes with it. And that is where the extreme danger lies since Paul is making a case in Romans 5 for God's *solution* to sin and death, which is Christ dying in our place on the cross.

People who claim to be Christians but reject Genesis (or portions of it) will quickly object to what I'm saying. They will claim that they do, in fact, believe that Jesus came and died for our sins on the cross, however they don't fully embrace the Creation account in Genesis.

What they don't realize is that by rejecting Genesis, the Creation account, and the origin of sin — they have eliminated the *need* for Christ's substitutionary death. If, as Paul argues in Romans 5, man is *not* responsible for sin, then there was *no need* for Jesus to come and represent the guilt of man by taking on human flesh. The incarnation of Christ becomes completely unnecessary because man is *not* responsible for death — God is!

The implications of rejecting a literal Genesis account are absolutely devastating to the Bible's main message — Jesus.

And every reference to God one day eliminating death and restoring His creation to its original state (without death) becomes a sham.

Finally, Jesus Himself is made out to be a perpetrator of lies. Since the account of the Global Flood is included in the first 11 chapters of Genesis (which is considered by such people to be part of the Bible's allegorical section), and since Jesus spoke of the Flood as an actual historical event (see Matthew 24:38), He is made out to be a liar and nothing less.

Do the dietary laws in Leviticus still apply to believers today?

Let's take a look at what the New Testament has to say concerning the food laws.

In Mark's Gospel account, Jesus was speaking to the religious leaders about their requirements for ceremonial washing. They believed that if they didn't wash their hands in the prescribed manner, they would defile their food and thus *become* defiled. After recording that conversation, Mark went on to write:

And when he had entered the house and left the people, his disciples asked him about the parable. And he said to them, "Then are you also without understanding? Do you not see that whatever goes into a person from outside cannot defile him, since it enters not his heart but his stomach, and is expelled?" (Thus he declared all foods clean.) (Mark 7:17–19)

The point of our Lord's remarks was to say that true obedience issues forth from a heart that loves God and not from the outward acts of keeping dietary laws. True holiness is internal. But just in case anyone might have missed the point, Mark further wrote, "**Thus he declared all foods clean.**"

Additionally, we have the narrative in Acts 10 which tells of Peter's vision from heaven in which he was specifically told to violate the Levitical dietary laws. Would the Lord have told Peter to do that if those dietary laws were still in force? (See Acts 10:9–15.)

Finally we have the Apostle Paul's clear statement recorded in his letter to the Romans where he declares, "**you are not under law but under grace**" (Romans 6:14).

In conclusion, it's impossible for the dietary laws to still be in force for us since believers are not under the Mosaic Law.

Why were concubines allowed in Old Testament times?

That's an excellent question, but one that is difficult to answer decisively. Here's what we know for sure:

1. When God created Adam, he was presented with one wife.

2. The first act of polygamy (recorded in Genesis 4) was committed by a descendant of Cain named Lamech. Scripture specifically records the fact that "Lamech married two women, one named Adah and the other Zillah" (Genesis 4:19).

3. We know that several individuals in the Bible such as Abraham, Jacob, David, and Solomon had multiple wives.

4. Finally, we also know that when Jesus came and spoke on the subject of marriage, He affirmed God's original intent that "the two shall become one flesh" (Matthew 19:5) — thus returning us to the divine model of one woman and one man.

So why was the taking of concubines and multiple wives allowed for a time? The fact is, we don't know, and God didn't include an explanation in the Bible. Although we're left with some questions, we can at least be confident in knowing that God's original plan for marriage involved one woman and one man.

Why did people live so long in the Old Testament?

That's a good question, and I need to start by saying that nowhere in the Bible does God specifically say *why* life spans were shortened. But let's start with what we *do* know.

1. Man was originally created to *never* die — death was introduced through sin and was never part of God's created order or plan for mankind. Death is an intruder and God refers to it as an "enemy" (1 Corinthians 15:26). Since man was created to live forever, it doesn't seem strange *at all* to think that lifespans could have been nearly 1,000 years.

OLD TESTAMENT AND THE LAW OF MOSES   193

2. Obviously, the gene pool has had a long time to become corrupted. Back before the Global Flood, people could do things like marrying a close family member without having to deal with significant risks. To do this in our day is to invite genetic difficulties but when the gene pool was younger, people often married within their family units. So, we know that from a purely genetic standpoint we are dealing with limitations today that did *not* exist at an earlier time.

3. In Scripture we see that lifespans began to decline sharply after the Global Flood. Why? Well, that's where we have to use some reason and even a little guesswork because the Bible doesn't say. But BibleStudy.org has some interesting information on the subject:

The earth after the flood was dramatically different than it was before. The differences included the altering of the climate, atmospheric changes, changes in the hydrologic cycle, geologic features, a significant increase in harmful radiation reaching ground level, man's dietary habits went from solely plant-based to one where meat was eaten, and so on. These and many other factors led to man's much shorter lifespans.

The first century historian Josephus asserts that man, at one time, did live very long lifespans. He attributes their longevity to God's mercy and the fact that the food they ate was much better at extending their years on earth than it was after the [flood]. (Antiquities of the Jews, Book 1, Chapter 3).*

In keeping with what is mentioned above, I believe the Global Flood did a *lot* more than just wipe out all life from the earth so God could start over with Noah and his family. I believe it altered the landscape of the earth in such a way that the sun's radiation now has a more profound effect on the aging process. But again, that's just my opinion. All we really know is that God allowed people to live much longer lifespans early on and then, for purposes He does not share with us, those lifespans were drastically reduced.

*BibleStudy.org. "Why Did Man Live Longer before the Flood?"

Why was the Day of Atonement necessary for Israel if sacrifices were being made daily?

That's an excellent question. The daily sacrifices and the annual Day of Atonement conveyed two different aspects of forgiveness. While the Day of Atonement represented salvation (being saved), the daily sacrifices represented our everyday need for cleansing.

This same question could be asked from a New Testament perspective: *If all my sins, past, present, and future are forgiven when I put my faith in Jesus, why then did He teach us to pray, "Forgive us our trespasses"?*

The fact is, once we come to Christ, we are still in need of daily cleansing for the sake of our relationship with the Lord. We don't confess our sins so that we will be saved over and over. We confess them so that nothing is standing in the way of our communion with our heavenly Father.

This was also depicted at the Last Supper when Jesus washed the disciple's feet. He said to them, "The one who has bathed does not need to wash, except for his feet, but is completely clean" (John 13:10). When we come to Christ, we are bathed by our trust in the person and work of Jesus on the cross — and in a sense, we are made clean completely, once for all. But we still walk every day through a dark and dirty world which requires us to wash our feet. Again, this is a picture of the daily sacrifices of the Old Testament and the directive to ask God to "forgive us our trespasses."

Chapter 12

THE HOLY TRINITY

- What specific verses explain the Trinity? 197

- How do I respond to God, Jesus, and the Holy Spirit? 198

- What is "Oneness" theology and why is it wrong? 199

What specific verses explain the Trinity?

There are no verses in the Bible that explain the Trinity. This is because the Trinity defies human explanation. However, there are many passages in God's Word where the Trinity is revealed.

One God
It is clear from the Bible that there is only one God. That is clear enough from passages such as Deuteronomy 6:4, Isaiah 43:10, and 1 Timothy 2:5, among others. There are not two, three, or more – there is just *one* God.

Three Persons
The next thing that is clearly revealed in Scripture is that there are three Persons who are all called "God" and are shown to have attributes that could only be possessed by God. Those three Persons are revealed as God the Father (John 6:27), Jesus Christ the Son (Colossians 1:16–17), and the Holy Spirit (John 14:26).

Some Bible passages refer to all three Persons in the same thought, such as the following:

...according to the foreknowledge of God the Father, in the sanctification of the Spirit, for obedience to Jesus Christ and for sprinkling with his blood: May grace and peace be multiplied to you. (1 Peter 1:2)

Notice Peter speaks of the Father, the Spirit, and the Son (Jesus Christ) all in one thought. This can also be seen in the following passage:

The grace of the Lord Jesus Christ and the love of God and the fellowship of the Holy Spirit be with you all. (2 Corinthians 13:14)

The doctrine of the Trinity reveals that the Father is God, the Son is God, and the Holy Spirit is God — and yet there is only **one** God. That is the essence of what the Bible reveals concerning the nature of God. Belief in the Trinity is a huge stretch for a lot of people — mostly owing to the fact that it extends beyond the range of our human comprehension. There are a lot of people who struggle to embrace anything they cannot grasp on an intellectual level. That's unfortunate since they are essentially demanding that God's nature must be understandable in order to be believed.

A very wise Bible teacher once told me that whenever I'm dealing with God, I should always leave room for mystery. I have found that to be incredibly helpful advice.

How do I respond to God, Jesus, and the Holy Spirit?

The functions of the members of the Godhead are specific, and yet there is *nothing* that one member of the Trinity does that the other two are not also involved with. Much of what happens to us as Christians (physically and spiritually) is through the agency of the Holy Spirit. He is the One who indwells us, witnesses to us, empowers us, convicts us, seals us, gives us spiritual gifts, and brings forth fruit in our lives. And yet the Holy Spirit is called "The Spirit of God" and "the Spirit of Jesus." They are One.

Concerning how or to whom you pray, I think you need to be careful not to overthink the nature of God. The distinctions within the Trinity are highlighted for the purpose of our study and understanding, but we must be careful not to make too much of them. We worship and serve **one** God and addressing Him ought to be consistent with that reality.

In the Word we are told to pray to the Father (Matthew 6:9), in Jesus' name (John 14:13), and in the power and leading of the Holy Spirit (Romans 8:26–27). However, we are not forbidden in the Word from addressing any Person of the Trinity. Once in a while, I will pray on a Sunday morning asking the Holy Spirit to open our eyes to the Word, but it would be just as appropriate to ask God to send His Spirit to do that work among us. On other occasions I have prayed, "Jesus, open us to Your Word so that we can see what You want us to see." Again, the work of opening our understanding is always through the agency of the Holy Spirit, but who we address specifically isn't really important. Because God is one, not just in purpose but also in essence, we are addressing *all three* Persons at any given time.

What is "Oneness" theology and why is it wrong?

Put simply, Oneness theology teaches that God is one person who manifests himself in three different modes — sometimes as God the Father, other times as God the Son, and sometimes as the Holy Spirit. Oneness (also called "modalism" or "Sabellianism") is known more commonly by the name "Jesus Only" since adherents of this teaching usually believe the name of "the One God" who is Jesus.

This teaching is traced back to the late 2nd and early 3rd

centuries when two men, Praxeas and Sabellius, popularized and propagated this theological idea. Such teachings have always been considered aberrant and heretical by the Christian church at large and that is because Oneness teaching flies in the face of clear biblical revelation.

The Bible reveals that there is One God who is revealed within the pages of Scripture in three Persons — Father, Son, and Holy Spirit. Even in the opening pages of the Word we are privileged to overhear a conversation between these three Persons at the time of Creation:

Then God said, "Let us make man in our image, after our likeness. And let them have dominion over the fish of the sea and over the birds of the heavens and over the livestock and over all the earth and over every creeping thing that creeps on the earth." So God created man in his own image, in the image of God he created him; male and female he created them. (Genesis 1:26–27)

And, at the baptism of Jesus by John, we are shown all three Persons of the Godhead at once as the Son emerges from the water and the Father's voice is heard from heaven while the Spirit descends on the Son in the form of a dove (see Mark 1:9–11; John 1:32–34).

In his book, *The Knowledge of the Holy*, A.W. Tozer writes:

Our sincerest effort to grasp the incomprehensible mystery of the Trinity must remain forever futile, and only by deepest reverence can it be saved from actual presumption.

(See also Matthew 28:19; 1 Peter 1:2)

Chapter 13

GOD

- How can I know that God exists? 202

- Is it necessary to prove God's existence? 204

- Where did sin and evil come from? 205

- If God created everything, did He also create pain, wars, natural disasters, and other bad things in the world? 206

- Why does God allow so much suffering in the world? 208

- Does God respect man's freewill? 209

- Does God change His mind? 211

- What does it mean to take God's name in vain? 212

How can I know that God exists?

God has given humans the capacity to know that something exists even if we can't know *how* that thing exists. For example, I can know that there is such a thing as timelessness (eternity) and yet, as a creature of time, I also understand that I cannot point to anything in my life experience that displays the characteristics of eternity. In fact, everything around me is just as much a prisoner of time as I am. So, how do I know that there is such a thing as eternity? Simply because God communicates it to me in His Word and I accept it on faith. Ecclesiastes 3:11 says that God "**has put eternity into man's heart.**" It's in our hearts, and not in our minds that we might comprehend it. We must leave room for that as a mystery of God.

If I say that eternity cannot exist simply because I cannot comprehend such a thing, I would essentially be declaring my mind to be the greatest thing in the universe, and anything outside or beyond my mind cannot possibly exist and is therefore untrue. To have such a mindset is the height of human arrogance.

The existence of God is somewhat easier to establish because unlike eternity, God has left His fingerprints on everything that we can see in our daily experience. The Apostle Paul explains that God's "**invisible attributes, namely, his eternal power and divine nature, have been clearly perceived, ever since the creation of the world, in the things that have been made**" (Romans 1:20). The reason they are "clearly perceived" is because God has also given all of humankind the ability to recognize and distinguish that which is the creation of a designer from that which is the by-product of random forces. For example, if an earthquake knocked our Scrabble board game off the shelf and onto the floor, I would look at the arrangement of the letters and I would know that the game ended up on the floor because of a random event. The very way the letters were sprawled on the floor would make that obvious. However, if I found all the letters from the Scrabble game on the floor arranged in such a way as to spell out a specific message to me, with each word spelled correctly, I would know that this was the work of a designer. Why? Because random events of disorder never result in order and intelligence.

I've spoken with many people who struggle to accept that God is a Trinity — one God and three Persons — because they cannot fathom how that could even be possible. But what they fail to realize is that if they *could* fathom the nature of God, their mind would be *equal* to the nature of God. But for God to be God, He must be above all and that means He must also be greater than man. And if God is greater than man, then it is logical to believe that His nature is also greater than man's ability to comprehend.

At the end of the day we have to come to terms with the fact that we are finite human beings that cannot comprehend what is incomprehensible. God, the uncreated Creator of all things, has expressed it in His Word to us when He says, "**For my thoughts are not your thoughts, neither are your ways my ways, declares the LORD. For as the heavens are higher than the earth, so are my ways higher than your ways and my thoughts than your thoughts**" (Isaiah 55:8–9).

The Apostle Paul expressed it this way: "*Oh, the depth of the riches and wisdom and knowledge of God! How unsearchable are his judgments and how inscrutable his ways!*" (Romans 11:33)

Is it necessary to prove God's existence?

There is nothing in Scripture that requires believers to prove the existence of God. In fact, the Bible itself never sets out to prove God's existence. It starts off with a plain and straightforward declaration found in Genesis 1:1, "**In the beginning God.**"

Furthermore, in the Psalms, the Holy Spirit moved upon David to write about God's existence saying, "**The heavens declare the glory of God, and the sky above proclaims his handiwork**" (Psalm 19:1). This verse tells us that we don't have to prove anything about the existence of God because Creation itself is constantly testifying about its Creator. This proclamation is so convincing that the Apostle Paul wrote that all men are without excuse.

For what can be known about God is plain to them, because God has shown it to them. For his invisible attributes, namely, his eternal power and divine nature, have been clearly perceived, ever since the creation of the world, in the things that have been made. So they are without excuse. (Romans 1:19–20)

The Bible speaks of defending and confirming the Gospel (see Philippians 1:7), but not God's existence. If someone chooses not to believe in a Creator God, it is because they have chosen to close their eyes to the evidence all around them.

Where did sin and evil come from?

The origin of evil can be a challenging subject. Because God is entirely pure and without sin, we know evil did not originate from Him. We also know that God is the Creator and Source of all things and one of His created beings was in fact, an angel that we now call Satan or the devil, from whom all sin and evil originates.

God granted to Satan, as well as the other angelic beings, the same power to create that He Himself possesses. But in Satan's case, he didn't merely create something — he originated that which is wholly at odds with God's own nature: the existence of evil. This is confirmed by some information our Lord Jesus gave us while speaking of Satan:

You are of your father the devil, and your will is to do your father's desires. He was a murderer from the beginning, and does not stand in the truth, because there is no truth in him. When he lies, he speaks out of his own character, for he is a liar and the father of lies. (John 8:44)

Notice that Jesus referred to Satan as "**a liar and the father of lies**." When the Bible makes mention of someone as the "father" of something, it is describing that person as the originator or starting point of that particular thing. For example, Abraham is called "the Father of the Jews" since the Jewish race began with him (Luke 1:73; Romans 4:1). Since Satan is "the father of lies" we know that he is the originator of lies and deception. How? We aren't told since no evil existed before, but that is what makes Satan so evil — he literally created evil.

The prophetic book of Ezekiel gives us this insightful information about Satan:

You were an anointed guardian cherub. I placed you; you were on the holy mountain of God; in the midst of the stones of fire you walked. You were blameless in your ways from the day you were created, till unrighteousness was found in you. (Ezekiel 28:14–15)

The origin of sin is a fascinating study, but all biblical evidence points to Satan as the mysterious originator of sin, untruth, and deception.

If God created everything, did He also create pain, wars, natural disasters, and other bad things in the world?

Most misunderstandings concerning God stem from our natural assumptions. Since God is "the Creator" people naturally assume that He created everything that exists today — including things like disease, war, and natural disasters. But that is not the case.

It is true that the Bible explicitly says that "God created all things" (Ephesians 3:9; Revelation 4:11), but these references point to the six days of Creation as recorded in Genesis 1–2. After each of those days of Creation we are told that God looked at all He had made and pronounced it to be "good." That obviously leaves us with the profound issue of explaining the existence of all the "bad" things we see in our world today. (The origin of evil has been a favorite subject of philosophers throughout the centuries.)

Genesis 3 explains the origin of all that you and I consider bad and evil, and it all begins with the introduction of sin into the world. The Bible tells us that with sin came death. That means physical death was not a part of God's original Creation. He never intended man to suffer the ravages of old age, sickness, disease, and all the accompanying ills that go with sin. Technically speaking, man created those things by *choosing* to fall into sin.

The Apostle Paul wrote to the Christians in Rome saying, "just as sin entered the world through one man, and death through sin, and in this way death came to all men" (Romans 5:12 NIV84). This passage agrees with the narrative of Genesis, reminding us that death was the result when sin came into the world.

Your question is one that people need to tackle and correctly address because of these reasons:

First, without a proper understanding of the origin of sin and death, we see a twisted and perverted image of the character and purpose of God. Instead of a loving and caring Creator, we see Him as One who inflicts the worst conditions upon His unsuspecting creation, filling their lives with pain, darkness, and hopelessness. (That certainly isn't a God I would want to worship!)

Secondly, when we understand that everything we see around us is "bad" as a result of sin, we are now ready to recognize the reason God sent His Son to this earth. Jesus came for the expressed purpose of overturning the dominion of sin and death. This He did by bearing the penalty of sin and conquering it by rising from the dead.

Why does God allow so much suffering in the world?

This question takes on many forms, but essentially it centers around why an all-powerful, loving, and kind God would allow evil and suffering to exist as part of our human experience.

People ask this question because they assume that since God is the Creator, He must have created suffering and death since these two things are so prevalent in our daily lives. But the fact is, the world we live in is "fallen" — corrupted and polluted — and it contains many things that are *not* part of God's original design.

The Bible tells us that God never intended the world to include sin, suffering, and evil. Even death wasn't part of God's plan for mankind. All those things came about as a result of man's rebellion against God. Ultimately, we have no one to blame for suffering and evil but ourselves.

In order for God to rid the world of suffering, He would have to abolish all sin. And to do that He would need to eliminate all sinners — which kind of defeats the point since no one would be around to enjoy this new sin-free world.

But that doesn't mean that God isn't working to eliminate suffering and death. In fact, He has already begun the process by sending His Son to pay the penalty of our sin through His death on the cross. You see, before the *consequences* of sin can be dealt with, the *penalty* of sin had to be taken care of first.

The death and subsequent resurrection of Jesus have set in motion the events that will eventually bring about God's plan to completely eliminate sin, suffering, and death. The promise to accomplish this is scattered all throughout the pages of Scripture. And as for the next event in God's redemptive timetable — it's none other than the return of Jesus Christ for His Bride, the Church.

So why is God taking so long? The Apostle Peter responds to that question this way:

The Lord is not slow in keeping his promise, as some understand slowness. He is patient with you, not wanting anyone to perish, but everyone to come to repentance. (2 Peter 3:9 NIV84)

This means God is giving mankind time to take advantage of the wonderful promise of forgiveness He has made available to all who will accept it.

When you're talking to unbelievers about God's plan to redeem this fallen world, don't forget to ask them if they have accepted God's offer of forgiveness through His Son. This is our hope, and we need to share it while there's still time.

Does God respect man's freewill?

The divinely respected free will of man is everywhere implied in the Bible, especially in passages such as:

"...**choose this day whom you will serve**..." (Joshua 24:15)

"**If anyone thirsts, let him come to me and drink.**" (John 7:37)

"**Come now, let us reason together, says the LORD**..." (Isaiah 1:18)

The numerous appeals to mankind through both the Old and New Testaments clearly communicate that God not only honors our free will choices, but He actually refuses to force Himself on anyone. Instead, He calls to those who are willing to listen and respond.

Consider the following two passages as proof that God respects the free will determinations of mankind:

The Lord is…not wishing that any should perish… (2 Peter 3:9)

"…**the way is easy that leads to destruction, and those who enter by it are many**." (Matthew 7:13)

In the first passage, the Apostle Peter explains that God is not willing that any should perish. And yet, Jesus reminds us that those who choose the path of destruction "**are many**." Clearly God honors the free will choices of mankind even when those choices are contrary to His own perfect will.

I've been asked many times over the years why God allowed Satan into the Garden to tempt Adam and Eve. The answer centers around this very issue of mankind's free will. At some point, Adam and Eve simply had to be tested to see which way they would choose to go. I suppose God could have created Adam and Eve as puppets or automatons who fulfilled His bidding without question, but it is clear He wished for all who come to Him to do so freely and of their own choosing.

The gift of free will is what uniquely sets us apart from the rest of created life and is the key to understanding what it means to be created in the image of God.

GOD   211

Does God change His mind?

There are certainly challenging passages in the Bible that seem to depict this idea of God changing His mind. Let's take 1 Samuel 15 for example.

The word of the LORD came to Samuel: "I regret that I have made Saul king..." (vv. 10–11)

"...the Glory of Israel will not lie or have regret, for he is not a man, that he should have regret." (v. 29)

And the LORD regretted that he had made Saul king over Israel. (v. 35b)

In one single chapter we're told that God regretted, and a few verses later that God does not have regrets. Are we looking at an honest-to-goodness contradiction in the Bible?

It sure appears so, except for two very important things:

First, you'll notice that this apparent "contradiction" occurs within the same narrative. Typically, when you find a contradiction in someone's writing, the two opposing statements are separated by several pages or chapters, giving the author time to forget that he or she has made two incompatible statements. But in this case, the remarks that seem contrary are almost back-to-back. I believe this shows that the author intentionally made these statements and did so without any concern about them contradicting one another.

Secondly, we must be very careful whenever typical human emotions or reactions are ascribed to God. Things like regret and remorse are common to us but that's because we make decisions with no guarantee about how they will work out. God, on the other hand, never wonders how His actions will work out and He's never surprised by any outcome.

In the case of King Saul, God knew ahead of time that Saul would falter in his responsibilities as king of Israel. However, the Lord's response to the situation had to be expressed in terms that humans would easily understand, therefore words like *regret* are used. This is called an "anthropomorphism," which is the attribution of a human characteristic or behavior to God. Many times, the Bible describes God's emotional responses in human-like terms, but we should never assume that God is just like us. It is technically impossible for God to experience regret the same way we do because He is never surprised or caught off guard. He knows exactly what will happen and He always has a plan.*

We need to understand that God's foreknowledge does not predetermine our outcome. The fact that He knows something will take place doesn't necessarily mean He caused that thing to happen.

What does it mean to take God's name in vain?

The prohibition against taking the Lord's name in vain is included in the Ten Commandments and is recorded in Exodus 20:7 which says:

"You shall not take the name of the LORD your God in vain, for the LORD will not hold him guiltless who takes his name in vain."

To fully understand this commandment, we need to realize that God's Name is so much *more* than just a title. The name of God is a declaration of His very being and character, and to use His name is to speak of who He is. Exodus 33 records a time when God passed by and proclaimed His name 'The LORD' to Moses (v.19) who was hidden in the cleft of the rock. We see here that God literally proclaimed His character to Moses.

The word *vain* means "empty" or "meaningless." We take God's name "in vain" when we use His name aimlessly. Even an expression like "Oh my God!" falls under this kind of use.

When I was a kid, taking the Lord's name in vain meant using God's name as a curse word. And no doubt that's included in the prohibition, but for the Jews it was connected to swearing a vow in the name of the Lord in an insincere or hypocritical manner. To make a vow invoking the Lord's name and then to not keep that vow was considered taking the Lord's name in vain. That's not something that happens much in our culture today.

The bottom line is that when we use God's name, it ought to be for prayer, praise, or personal sharing; and it should always be spoken with respect and honor. In other words, our speech should reflect our heart toward God.

Chapter 14

JESUS

- Why are the genealogies of Jesus different in Matthew and Luke? 215

- Why did Jesus pray to God if they are equal? 216

- Why did Jesus refer to Himself as the "Son of Man"? 217

- Is Jesus always willing to heal physically all that come to Him? 219

- Did Jesus actually drink fermented wine, or only grape juice? 220

- Was Jesus crucified on a 'cross' or a 'tree'? 222

- How could Jesus be with the thief in paradise on the day of His crucifixion, if on the following Sunday He told Mary He had "not yet ascended to the Father"? 223

- Did Jesus really descend into hell? 225

- Was Jesus the only one to ascend into heaven? 227

- Did Jesus ever get sick? 229

Why are the genealogies of Jesus different in Matthew and Luke?

I personally believe that Luke is giving our Lord's maternal genealogy through Mary. This position is based on clues rather than proof, yet I believe those clues are compelling.

Matthew and Luke each give a different name for the father of Joseph. Matthew says Joseph's father was Jacob (Matthew 1:16), while Luke says it was Heli (Luke 3:23). Since the Jews were extremely careful when recording genealogies, it seems highly unlikely that these two men just got it wrong, especially since they were dealing with a name that was only one generation removed. So, how do we explain this?

My belief is that since there was no specific Koine Greek word for "son-in-law," Joseph was called the "son of Heli" by marriage to Mary — which means Mary was Heli's daughter. Also, Luke speaks of Jesus being the son of Joseph, "as was supposed" (Luke 3:23). The other clue that leads us to believe that Luke is recording Mary's genealogy is the fact that no other Gospel writer gives more information about Jesus' life as a child. It seems very likely that Luke spent time with Mary getting details that could have come from no other source.

The benefit of recording both Mary's and Joseph's family lineage is that Jesus is seen as the legitimate son of David whether determined by law through Joseph (as recorded by Matthew) or by blood through Mary (as seen in Luke). Some people object to this conclusion based on the fact that tracing someone's genealogy through a woman was extremely rare. I agree...but a virgin birth is even more rare!

Why did Jesus pray to God if they are equal?

There's nothing surprising about struggling with the mystery and majesty of the incarnation, but this question reveals faulty reasoning. For starters, it includes the assumption that prayer implies subordination on the part of the one praying. It further assumes that subordination equals inferiority. The conclusion is that if Jesus prayed to His Father, He was therefore subordinate to God; ergo, inferior to God.

Here's what so many people forget:

1. As the Son of Man, Jesus willingly subordinated Himself to the Father. In his letter to the Philippians, the Apostle Paul wrote that "**though** [Jesus] **was in the form of God**, [He] **did not count equality with God a thing to be grasped, but emptied himself, by taking the form of a servant**" (Philippians 2:6–7).

That passage is full of vital information. It tells us that:

- Jesus was in the form of God prior to His incarnation.

- Jesus did not consider His equality with the Father something to be held on to.

- Jesus emptied Himself.

That last point means Jesus' subordination to the Father in no way implies or suggests an inferiority of nature. His was a willing subordination, not a mandatory one.

2. The Apostle John tells us that the living Word of God became a man in the Person of Jesus Christ and came to live His life on earth *as a man* (see John 1:1,14). As such, He addressed His heavenly Father as any man would. The fact

that He prayed to God the Father takes nothing from His own deity.

3. Jesus came to *model* all aspects of the Christian life, and prayer was certainly one of them.

God the Father and God the Son are separate Persons. As such, they have been in communication from all eternity. The communion they shared during Jesus' earthly sojourn was just a continuation of that closeness and fellowship. It took the form of prayer simply because Jesus took the form of man.

Why did Jesus refer to Himself as the "Son of Man"?

Jesus never explained why He liked to use the title "Son of Man" during His earthly ministry but as we dig into the Word, we find some very enlightening clues, one of which is recorded for us in the book of Daniel.

"I saw in the night visions, and behold, with the clouds of heaven there came one like a son of man, and he came to the Ancient of Days and was presented before him. And to him was given dominion and glory and a kingdom, that all peoples, nations, and languages should serve him; his dominion is an everlasting dominion, which shall not pass away, and his kingdom one that shall not be destroyed." (Daniel 7:13-14)

This prophecy is quite clearly about the coming of the Messiah — one who is "**given dominion and glory and a kingdom**." And yet he was seen by Daniel as "**one like a son of man**."

The title "Son of Man" points to the humanity of the One who "became flesh and dwelt among us" (John 1:14). Jesus came to the earth to represent sinful man both in life and on the cross where He bore our sins. That role of representation was one that Jesus consistently expressed throughout His earthly ministry, beginning with His baptism in the Jordan River by John.

You will remember that John's baptism was a baptism of repentance (Acts 19:4) and yet Jesus insisted that He should be baptized. We know He was without sin, so why should the sinless Son of God be baptized for repentance? That's because in doing so, Jesus was identifying with sinful mankind.

Believers should never allow the title "Son of Man" to give them a moment's concern that somehow Jesus never claimed to be equal with God. In fact, there were times where Jesus referred to Himself as the "Son of Man" while also making definitive claims of deity:

"When the Son of Man comes in his glory, and all the angels with him, then he will sit on his glorious throne." (Matthew 25:31)

"But I tell you, from now on you will see the Son of Man seated at the right hand of Power and coming on the clouds of heaven." (Matthew 26:64)

(Notice how this last verse connects directly with the passage in Daniel quoted above.)

The title "Son of Man" was used by Jesus to emphasize His humanity. It causes no problems with embracing Jesus as God. He is simply God in human flesh.

Is Jesus always willing to heal physically all that come to Him?

This question usually centers around a statement recorded in Luke 5. When approached by a man with leprosy who said, "Lord, if you will, you can make me clean" (v. 12), Jesus replied saying, "I will" (v. 13). This response is often rendered in other translations as "I am willing" and has led many to conclude that since Jesus never changes, His statement is always true for every person who approaches Him for physical healing.

I've always been fascinated by our capacity for taking a single statement from our Lord and applying it as an absolute rule for all times and all people. We make huge assumptions which I don't believe are always warranted from a biblical perspective.

The problem with making the first assumption from Luke 5:13 – that Jesus is always willing to heal – is that it leads to other assumptions *if*, and *when* the healing isn't manifested as we expected. We quickly look for a reason as to why our prayers were not answered and accusations begin to fly about unconfessed sin or a lack of faith. These sorts of rash conclusions bring condemnation and deep distress.

I am reminded of Isaiah 55:8–9 which says:

For my thoughts are not your thoughts, neither are your ways my ways, declares the LORD. For as the heavens are higher than the earth, so are my ways higher than your ways and my thoughts than your thoughts.

This passage serves as a constant reminder that God's ways and thoughts are infinitely above our own and we would be wise to never assume to know His specific direction for any situation. I try whenever possible to leave God's sovereign will entirely in His hands and not to presume upon it with my own thoughts and demands.

That said, I believe in healing and I believe God is *always* good. But I also believe that my definition of "good" is limited by my own circumstances and my own understanding.

Did Jesus actually drink fermented wine, or only grape juice?

In the history of the Christian faith, certain taboos have risen to the surface and for many believers, one of the worst is the consumption of alcohol. For them, to do so is sin, simple as that. And since Jesus never committed sin, the natural conclusion is that He never tasted fermented drink.

There's only one problem with that conclusion: It doesn't square with God's Word. Let's check our facts.

Fact #1: Drinking alcohol is *nowhere* condemned in the Word of God. (But the Bible does passionately condemn drunkenness — overindulgence to the point of intoxication.) In fact, the Apostle Paul even counseled Timothy to take "a little wine" because of his stomach ailments (1 Timothy 5:23). Notice Paul counseled "a little." He would never suggest that Timothy drink to excess because that was strictly forbidden for obvious reasons* (see Ephesians 5:18). Sometimes potable water was hard to find, and this made drinking other beverages necessary. Culturally, wine was an accepted drink although the dangers of overindulgence were known and are certainly addressed in God's Word.

Fact #2: The first recorded miracle performed by our Lord took place in Cana of Galilee where He turned water into wine at a wedding feast. (Believe me, they did *not* serve their guests grape juice at a wedding feast.) The belief that Jesus never tasted fermented drink is based on the presupposition that drinking in any amount is a sin. But since the Bible doesn't support that conclusion, there is absolutely no reason to believe Jesus never tasted fermented wine.

A Word of Caution to Believers

Now that I have addressed this question from a purely biblical standpoint, let me add a pastoral note. It is my considered opinion that believers today are altogether too casual about drinking and we need to prayerfully consider how our actions and attitudes may be affecting others.

Although I believe that Jesus most likely tasted fermented wine, there's one important thing to keep in mind: You're *not* Jesus – and the chances of alcohol messing up your life are pretty good! Wisdom would tell you to steer clear of anything that has the potential to cause problems.

As a pastor, I choose not to drink. Ever. Not because it's forbidden, but because it's imprudent. I have the freedom to drink, but I choose not to exercise my freedom because drinking has taken down much better men than I, and it would be foolish for me to think I am above that sort of destructive potential. Another compelling reason behind this personal choice is because I have a responsibility to live my life in a manner that considers my weaker brother who, at the sight of me drinking, might possibly be emboldened to do the same which could bring about his ruin.

As Paul said:

"All things are lawful," but not all things are helpful. "All things are lawful," but not all things build up. (1 Corinthians 10:23)

*To that I'd like to add another point: If a person cannot exercise self-control in the consumption of an alcoholic beverage, then it's far better to not partake at all. As King Solomon wrote, "Wine is a mocker, strong drink a brawler, and whoever is led astray by it is not wise" (Proverbs 20:1).

Was Jesus crucified on a 'cross' or a 'tree'?

The Bible uses both words. John records a scene from the crucifixion saying:

…but standing by the cross of Jesus were his mother and his mother's sister, Mary the wife of Clopas, and Mary Magdalene. (John 19:25)

But later, in Peter's first letter, we read:

He himself bore our sins in his body on the tree… (1 Peter 2:24)

So, which is it — a cross or a tree?

Well, technically speaking, Jesus was crucified on a cross made from wood which was taken from a tree. But Peter's use of the word "tree" goes far beyond simply explaining the composition of the cross. Even though he didn't quote it, Peter was thinking of a passage from the book of Deuteronomy

— a verse the Apostle Paul *does* quote in his letter to the Galatians. It goes like this:

Christ redeemed us from the curse of the law by becoming a curse for us—for it is written, "Cursed is everyone who is hanged on a tree." (Galatians 3:13)

The Jews knew from that statement in Deuteronomy that anyone hung on a tree was under a curse from God, and they came to understand that Jesus bore the curse of sin on our behalf through His sacrifice on the cross.

So, in summary, the words *cross* or *tree* don't matter at all in terms of identifying the instrument of crucifixion. But the word "tree" points back to Deuteronomy to help us understand the lengths that Jesus went to in order to save us from our sin.

How could Jesus be with the thief in paradise on the day of His crucifixion, if on the following Sunday He told Mary He had "not yet ascended to the Father"?

The statement that Jesus made to Mary at the open tomb has been the subject of much confusion. But it all centers around the fact that Mary had lost Jesus once and she wasn't about to lose Him again. That's why when she finally recognized Him there by the tomb, she grabbed onto Him and wasn't about to let go. Jesus then said to her, "Do not cling to me," which means, "It's okay Mary, I'm not going anywhere." He then went on to say, "for I have not yet ascended to the

Father" (John 20:17). That's the phrase that people struggle to understand because on the surface it sounds like Jesus was saying He had not yet been to heaven. But in the Greek, this phrase refers to a state of being rather than an action. In essence, Jesus was saying, "I have not yet entered into an ascended state."

Jesus was planning to spend the next 40 days (off and on) with the disciples before ultimately entering His final "ascended state." He was communicating to Mary that there was no need to hold on to Him because His final ascension was still many days away. He was *not* saying that He had not yet been in heaven.

A lot of people are curious about what Jesus was doing during that time when His physical body was in the tomb. I believe one of the tasks He had then was to bring to heaven those who had previously died in faith. We know that under the old covenant people did not ascend to heaven since "the way" had not yet been opened (see John 3:13). Believers were taken to a holding place which Jesus spoke about called "Abraham's bosom" (Luke 16:22). It was a place of comfort where they awaited the completion of our Lord's work on the cross so that heaven might finally be opened to them. How incredible that must have been for our Lord to usher those folks into the never-removed presence of God!

JESUS 225

Did Jesus really descend into hell?

The notion that Jesus descended into hell is a product of the Apostles' Creed — an early extra-biblical statement of Christian belief that is still used by believers as a type of statement of faith. It goes like this:

I believe in God the Father, Almighty, Maker of heaven and earth: And in Jesus Christ, his only begotten Son, our Lord: Who was conceived by the Holy Ghost, born of the Virgin Mary: Suffered under Pontius Pilate; was crucified, dead and buried: He descended into hell: The third day he rose again from the dead: He ascended into heaven, and sits at the right hand of God the Father Almighty: From thence he shall come to judge the quick and the dead: I believe in the Holy Ghost: I believe in the holy catholic church: the communion of saints: The forgiveness of sins: The resurrection of the body: And the life everlasting. Amen.

When the Apostles' Creed took its English form sometime in the 16th century, the Greek word *hades* was translated as "hell" even though the typical biblical word for hell was *gehenna*.

In Acts 2, Peter quoted David speaking prophetically concerning the Messiah. David said, "For you will not abandon my soul to Hades..." (v. 27). The word *hades* simply refers to the abode of the departed spirits which is why the NIV translates it as "grave." That is also why several English translations of the Apostles' Creed have changed that line to say, "he descended to the dead."

There is really nothing compelling in the Greek of the New Testament that would reveal that Christ descended into hell. In fact, if we cite Jesus' own words, we will remember that He promised the penitent thief that "today you will be with me in Paradise" (Luke 23:43). As for me, I'm more comfortable sticking with the Lord's own words to explain where He went after His crucifixion rather than some creed.

Some might argue that Ephesians 4:9 supports the Apostles' Creed since it speaks of Jesus descending "to the lower, earthly regions" (NIV). They assume this phrase refers to hell, but once again it could just as easily refer to the grave.

Others like to quote a passage from 1 Peter which speaks of Jesus preaching to "the spirits in prison" (3:18–19). This is considered one of the most difficult passages in the New Testament to understand. Add to that the fact that the specifics of when Jesus preached to the spirits in prison isn't at all made clear in the passage. To use these verses as a proof text that Jesus descended into hell is a dangerous walk on very thin ice.

So, is there danger in teaching that Jesus descended into hell? Why in the world would Jesus need to descend into a place of torment and suffering?

Some believe Jesus spent time in hell suffering torment on our behalf. But that would be completely inconsistent with our Lord's victorious cry from the cross when He declared, "It is finished," just before dismissing His Spirit (John 19:30). The words "It is finished" make up a common phrase heard in the marketplace when sellers would say "paid in full." To say that our Lord's suffering on the cross was somehow incomplete or needed additional time in hell is to open a theological can of worms.

Frankly, it's not far from the unbiblical idea of the Roman Catholic Mass where Jesus is believed to sacrifice Himself over and over at each Mass.

I have no doubt that the Apostles' Creed was worded in such

a way as to make it very clear that Jesus died in a genuine and literal manner. It was *not* meant to suggest or teach that the suffering of our Lord was extended beyond the cross, or that what He accomplished there was insufficient or incomplete.

Was Jesus the only one to ascend into heaven?

This is a commonly asked question since there's an account in 2 Kings that describes Elijah ascending into heaven. Then of course we also encounter passages which record the words of Jesus saying that no one has ascended into heaven except the One that came down. So, how do we sort this thing out?

Let's look at Jesus' words found in the Book of John:

No one has ascended into heaven except he who descended from heaven, the Son of Man. (John 3:13)

And yet the latter part of 2 Kings 2:11 clearly says:

And Elijah went up by a whirlwind into heaven.

Several attempts to explain this apparent contradiction have been made by Bible teachers and students of the Word, but quite honestly, none of them have come up with a satisfactory explanation. I believe the problem is not the text itself, but rather our limited understanding.

For starters, we know so little about heaven. In 2 Corinthians 12:2, the Apostle Paul writes about being taken up to the "third heaven." Good grief! We haven't even heard anything about a first or a second heaven! Paul doesn't attempt to explain himself and that means we are left with a mystery. I've heard some interesting theories attempting to define this third heaven, but in the end they are just guesses. We just don't know.

All we really know about the statement made in John 3:13 is that there was something completely unique about the ascension of Jesus. It was entirely unlike what happened to Elijah. But again, that's pretty much all we know.

Jesus told a story recorded in Luke 16 that spoke clearly of a holding place for those who died in faith. It wasn't heaven per se, but it was a place where we believe the righteous dead congregated prior to Jesus' death on the cross. It was only *after* His death and resurrection that we believe the gates of heaven were opened for us. This mysterious place may have been called "heaven" in an Old Covenant context.

The bottom line is that heaven is largely a mystery to us. We are in the dark on specific aspects of heaven and God has chosen to allow us to remain that way for His own reasons. What we *do* know is that the ascension of Jesus was entirely unique in that it had not been accomplished by any other person.

Did Jesus ever get sick?

Sickness and death entered the human condition when sin was introduced into God's otherwise perfect creation. Since then, mankind has been plagued with all sorts of sickness and ailments that eventually take their toll on our bodies and as a result, we expire physically.

The Bible does not say whether Jesus ever suffered a physical ailment. But as we consider this question, I think it's important to remember that while Jesus shared our humanity, He never gave in to sin. The writer to the Hebrews said:

For we do not have a high priest who is unable to sympathize with our weaknesses, but one who in every respect has been tempted as we are, yet without sin. (Hebrews 4:15)

Jesus experienced *all* our temptations, but He never gave in to sin. And because He was without sin, it is reasonable to assume that He did not suffer the effects of sin, like sickness. In fact, what we see in the Word is quite the opposite – when He touched the sick and infirmed, they were healed of their diseases.

Chapter 15

HOLY SPIRIT

- What is the baptism of the Holy Spirit? 231

- How do I know if I've been baptized with the Holy Spirit? 234

- What does it mean to blaspheme the Holy Spirit? 235

- Will God ever remove His Holy Spirit from me? 237

What is the baptism of the Holy Spirit?

We're told in the Bible that Jesus appeared to His disciples for a period of about 40 days after His resurrection and during one of those meetings, He exhorted them to wait for the coming work of the Spirit that would prepare them for ministry. Here's how it is recorded in the book of Acts:

And while staying with them he ordered them not to depart from Jerusalem, but to wait for the promise of the Father, which, he said, "you heard from me; for John baptized with water, but you will be baptized with the Holy Spirit not many days from now...you will receive power when the Holy Spirit has come upon you, and you will be my witnesses in Jerusalem and in all Judea and Samaria, and to the end of the earth." (Acts 1:4–5,8)

Jesus is the One who first used the phrase "baptized with the Holy Spirit" and He was very clear why the disciples needed to wait for it — they needed power. And that is what the baptism of the Spirit is all about: being empowered to be witnesses for Christ.

It is only after the baptism of the Spirit that we begin to see the activity of spiritual gifts. Prior to the baptism of the Spirit those gifts were not present in the lives of the disciples. It's clear that this is the "power" Jesus referred to when He told His disciples to wait in Jerusalem and that this power is the purpose behind believers being baptized by the Spirit.

I have identified five myths that are being perpetuated concerning the baptism of the Spirit:

Myth #1: The baptism and gifts of the Spirit are no longer for today.

This is called "Cessationism" and it is the belief that the gifts of the Holy Spirit have ceased to function in the church.

232 PASTOR, I HAVE A QUESTION

There is not one shred of biblical evidence to support the belief that the baptism of the Holy Spirit is not for present-day believers. We continue to need God's power to witness for Christ just like the believers did in the first century.

Myth #2: The baptism of the Spirit and the indwelling of the Spirit are one and the same thing — or we receive the baptism of the Spirit when we come to know Christ as Savior.

Not so. This is a confusion between the indwelling work of the Spirit and the baptism of the Spirit. When we put our faith in Jesus Christ for forgiveness, we receive God's Holy Spirit to indwell us. This is a once and for all work of God's Spirit. But throughout the book of Acts we see the followers of Jesus being repeatedly baptized and empowered by the Spirit. The indwelling work of the Spirit is for salvation while the baptism of the Spirit is for power — two very different works of the Spirit whose respective distinctions are emphasized in the Bible through the use of the prepositions "in" (indwelling) and "on" or "upon" (baptism of the Spirit).

Myth #3: The baptism of the Holy Spirit is the definitive sign of being born again.

Wrong. Jesus did not say, "You will be saved when the Holy Spirit has come upon you." What He said to the disciples was that they will "receive power when the Holy Spirit has come upon you" (Acts 1:8). It is very possible for someone to be saved and be a child of God and still not "receive power" through the baptism of the Spirit.

Myth #4: If you haven't spoken in tongues, you haven't been baptized by the Spirit.

This, I believe, is probably one of the most pervasive and troubling statements being perpetuated about the baptism of the Spirit. It creates an enormous pressure among Christians to prove they are just as spiritual as others and this results in a lot of "faking it." Christians write to me often asking if the gibberish they hear passing for "speaking in tongues" is genuine. These same people are belittled and rebuked by others for even asking the question and are told that if they had faith, they wouldn't question what they hear. (By the way, that's called "spiritual bullying.")

The gift of tongues is wonderful, but Jesus did not say that it was the final evidence of being baptized by the Holy Spirit. He said the real evidence is "power" which can manifest in many different ways or gifts — tongues being just one of them.

Myth #5: Those who are baptized in the Holy Spirit are more spiritual than those who are not.

This is fundamentally untrue. The believers at Corinth enthusiastically embraced the baptism of the Holy Spirit as well as all the accompanying gifts of the Spirit, and still the Apostle Paul referred to them as "people of the flesh" (1 Corinthians 3:1) who desperately needed to grow in spiritual maturity.

The baptism of the Holy Spirit is one of the most wonderful things God has given to the Church to enable and empower us to accomplish the work He has called us to do. I encourage believers to pray that they might be baptized with the Spirit and to do so often. We all need supernatural power from on high to shine the light of Christ in a very dark world.

234 PASTOR, I HAVE A QUESTION

How do I know if I've been baptized with the Holy Spirit?

A common issue when dealing with the baptism of the Holy Spirit is that people wonder if they've truly received it. Some Christian groups attempt to solve this by simply saying that if someone has been given the gift of tongues then that person has received it. The problem is, when people desperately seek and want to be baptized with the Spirit, they will do just about anything — including faking a spiritual gift — just to convince themselves and others that it truly happened.

Let me interject at this point that I have personally received this baptism including the gift of speaking in other tongues, and I wholeheartedly believe in the baptism of the Spirit as a thoroughly biblical truth. However, the overemphasis on receiving that *one* gift is not in keeping with the words of our Lord as recorded in Acts 1 where Jesus first spoke of the baptism of the Spirit. He not only used that specific term, telling His disciples they would be "baptized with the Holy Spirit" (Acts 1:5), but He also went on to describe how they would know they were recipients of this gift: "...you will receive power when the Holy Spirit has come upon you; and you will be my witnesses" (Acts 1:8).

I can think of no more authoritative description of the baptism of the Spirit than the one given by Jesus — it is all about receiving God's power to be His witness. Power, therefore, is the evidence of the baptism of the Spirit — *spiritual power.*

So, how do you know if you've received the baptism of the Holy Spirit? The same way you know you've received forgiveness of sins — *by faith.* Jesus promised that if you ask the Father, He would send His Holy Spirit (see Luke 11:13). Your responsibility is to receive that promise by faith and begin to walk it out. But remember this: the baptism of the Spirit is not about feeling better or stronger. It's about being empowered to be a witness for Jesus Christ. Again and again, we see believers in the book of Acts calling on God to give them His power to shine their light for Christ, and God met them every time (see Acts 4).

Start praying for the Lord to manifest His unlimited power in your life and to use that spiritual dynamic to build the Kingdom and glorify His Name. As you pray, ask the Lord to build your faith so that you can lay hold of His promises without wavering. Keep reading Luke 11 and Acts 1 and ask the Lord to imprint those promises on your heart.

What does it mean to blaspheme the Holy Spirit?

The word *blaspheme* means "to utter obscenity or profanity, or to speak things that are irreverent and untrue about God." The specific term in question, "blasphemy against the Spirit," is recorded in Matthew, Mark, and Luke. (See Matthew 12:31; Mark 3:29; Luke 12:10.)

Jesus mentioned blasphemy against the Spirit in relation to how the Pharisees were claiming that He was casting out demons through the agency and power of Satan. Jesus referred to speaking against the Holy Spirit as a sin that "will not be forgiven."

But more than what the religious leaders were saying is what they were doing — rejecting the testimony of the Holy

Spirit concerning the Person and work of Jesus. Since only the Holy Spirit can convict and ultimately change the heart of an unsaved person, the stubborn refusal to accept that revelation of who Jesus is removes any possibility for the saving work of the cross of Christ to be applied to that person's life.

Over the years I have spoken to many people who have been plunged into a paralyzing fear over the belief that they have somehow committed this unpardonable sin. But in each case, I have found that these people have not rejected the testimony of the Holy Spirit. In fact, they believe it with all their hearts and they believe Jesus died for their sins.

Many times these people struggle because they recall saying something reckless about the Holy Spirit and they fear they have committed this kind of blasphemy. I would like to respond to that idea by quoting Pastor David Guzik's comments on Luke 12:

...true blasphemy against the Spirit is more than a formula of words; it is a settled disposition of life that rejects the testimony of the Holy Spirit regarding Jesus. Even if someone has intentionally said such things, they can still repent and prevent a settled rejection of Jesus.

David Guzik, "Luke 12 — Attitudes for Followers of Jesus," EnduringWord.com.

Will God ever remove His Holy Spirit from me?

Let's start by establishing some helpful biblical facts:

Fact #1: God's Holy Spirit in the life of a believer is referred to as a "gift" (see Acts 2:38; 10:45).

Fact #2: God's gifts are irrevocable (see Romans 11:29).

This means that God's Spirit is *never* revoked in the life of a believer, even if we endure a period of backsliding. David's prayer of repentance in Psalm 51 may come to mind and you might wonder, "If that's the case, then why did David plead with God not to remove His Holy Spirit?" In that Psalm, he said: **"Cast me not away from your presence, and take not your Holy Spirit from me"** (v.11).

That passage sure makes it sound like God *does* remove His Spirit in cases of disobedience. David was concerned enough to ask the Lord *not* to do it.

But remember that David was living under a different dispensation of the Spirit than the one that applies to us today. For example, in David's day the Holy Spirit did not indwell a believer. He only came *upon* an individual to anoint and empower that person for service. Under the new covenant, the Holy Spirit comes not only *upon* but also *in* — to live inside or indwell. And since the facts stated above are made under the new covenant, our conclusion is that the gift of God's Holy Spirit in the life of a believer will *never* be revoked due to disobedience.

Chapter 16

LAST DAYS

- Will the Rapture take place before the Great Tribulation? 239

- Will all Israel be saved, or just a remnant? 240

- Who are the 144,000 in the Book of Revelation? 241

Will the Rapture take place before the Great Tribulation?

The Second Coming of Jesus occurs in two parts. The first is called the "Rapture," which is when Christ returns for His Bride (the Church). At the Rapture, Jesus will not literally return to the earth but will rather appear "in the clouds." This is why the Apostle Paul writes that we will rise to meet Him in the air (1 Thessalonians 4:17). This event will usher in the Great Tribulation which is described as a terrible time of suffering and hardship when God will pour out His wrath on the earth. The outpouring of God's wrath is precisely why I believe the Church will already be with the Lord before the Tribulation.

As Paul wrote, "**God has not destined us for wrath**" (1 Thessalonians 5:9).

After the seven-year Great Tribulation, Jesus will physically return to the earth along with the saints (the Church) and after destroying the enemies of Israel, He will reign upon the earth for a period of 1,000 years. This physical return is what is technically referred to as the Second Coming.

The Church has and will continue to experience all the hardships and difficulties associated with a fallen and rebellious world that is under the temporary control of Satan. Wars, famine, disasters, and all other forms of adversity and affliction are part of living in this world. Jesus even told us they will certainly be present and will even increase before His coming (see Matthew 24:6–8). But what the Church will *not* experience is the outpouring of God's wrath for reasons I've stated above.

At present, believers are already experiencing heightened persecution and there's no reason to believe this trend will subside before the Lord comes for us. If anything, I totally expect such things to persist and intensify. But these are the kinds of challenges Jesus told us to expect (see John 15:18–21).

So, will believers suffer hardships and persecutions? Yes. Will believers suffer the wrath of God? *Absolutely not.* Jesus already bore God's wrath for us on the cross.

Will all Israel be saved, or just a remnant?

All Israel will be saved on that day but by comparison with Israel's original numbers, those saved will be just a small remnant.

In Romans, Paul writes about the final condition of Israel *after* the Tribulation Period, which is referred to in Scripture as a "time of distress for Jacob" (Jeremiah 30:7). The latter half of the Tribulation will be a terrible time for the Jews, but when all hope seems lost, Jesus will return to the earth and deliver them from their enemies who are poised to destroy all Israel. When the Jews living on the earth see their Deliverer, they will recognize Him as the One "**whom they have pierced**." Zechariah tells us that they will "**mourn for him, as one mourns for an only child, and weep bitterly over him**" (Zechariah 12:10). Why is that? Because they will know for certain that He is Jesus — the One they previously rejected.

The upside is that Israel will celebrate their deliverance with a national conversion to Christ on that day because God will give them a spirit of grace to call upon the Lord. Zechariah wrote:

"On that day there shall be a fountain opened for the house of David and the inhabitants of Jerusalem, to cleanse them from sin and uncleanness..." (Zechariah 13:1)

That is what Paul meant by the words, "all Israel will be saved." But Isaiah reminds us that although their original numbers were "as the sand of the sea," those saved will be but a small remnant by comparison (Isaiah 10:22).

Who are the 144,000 in the Book of Revelation?

Let's look at the passage in question:

After this I saw four angels standing at the four corners of the earth, holding back the four winds of the earth, that no wind might blow on earth or sea or against any tree. Then I saw another angel ascending from the rising of the sun, with the seal of the living God, and he called with a loud voice to the four angels who had been given power to harm earth and sea, saying, "Do not harm the earth or the sea or the trees, until we have sealed the servants of our God on their foreheads." And I heard the number of the sealed, 144,000, sealed from every tribe of the sons of Israel: 12,000 from the tribe of Judah were sealed, 12,000 from the tribe of Reuben, 12,000 from the tribe of Gad, 12,000 from the tribe of Asher, 12,000 from the tribe of Naphtali, 12,000 from the tribe of Manasseh, 12,000 from the tribe of Simeon, 12,000 from the tribe of Levi, 12,000 from the tribe of Issachar, 12,000 from the tribe of Zebulun, 12,000

242   PASTOR, I HAVE A QUESTION

from the tribe of Joseph, 12,000 from the tribe of Benjamin were sealed. (Revelation 7:1–8)

What are the clues we see here that will help us determine the identity of these people?

Clue #1: The first clue as to their identity comes from verse 3 which says: "**Do not harm the earth or the sea or the trees, until we have sealed the servants of our God on their foreheads.**"

So they are "servants" of God. That's pretty simple.

Clue #2: If you read verses 4 through 8, you'll see that these people are Jews. The various tribes from which they descend are even given in the passage.

Clue #3: We go back to verse 3 and read that these Jewish servants are "**sealed...on their foreheads.**" People try to find some weird and sensational meaning to this seal, but there's nothing strange about it at all. Three times in his letters the Apostle Paul spoke of believers being "sealed" by the Holy Spirit (see 2 Corinthians 1:22; Ephesians 1:13; 4:30). This is common language for born-again believers. In the book of Revelation, the seal of the Lord was uniquely visible so that John might know without a doubt who these people were — Jews who had placed their faith in Jesus Christ.

And finally, **Clue #4** has to do with when these people appear on the scene. Revelation 7:1 simply begins with the words, "**After this...**"

After what? Well, the previous chapter ends with these ominous words: "**for the great day of their wrath has come, and who can stand?**" (Revelation 6:17). The great day of the Lord's wrath is, of course, the Great Tribulation. Therefore these 144,000 Jewish converts to Christianity will rise up sometime during the seven-year period that makes up the Great Tribulation.

To answer your question, the 144,000 in Revelation are Jews who will come to faith in Christ during the Great Tribulation.

Chapter 17

ON DEATH AND GOING TO HEAVEN

- Do children who die go to heaven? 245

- Do people become angels after they die? 247

- Do we enter a state of "soul sleep" after death? 250

- Do stillborn babies go to heaven? 252

- Can we talk to our departed loved ones? 253

- How will we recognize one another in heaven before we receive our new bodies? 255

Do children who die go to heaven?

The term "age of accountability" is often mentioned when addressing this question and while you won't find those words in the Bible, the idea that children are treated differently from adults is found in various passages throughout the Scriptures.

The first occurs when the people of Israel rebelled against God and refused to enter the Promised Land. God told them that all adults aged 20 years and over would die in the wilderness and never enter the Promised Land. This distinction in age popularized the idea that there exists in the heart of God a differentiation between the time when every person becomes accountable for their sin, and a period before such time when they are not culpable for their actions. Another reference found within the prophecies of Isaiah describes childhood as a time "**before [the child] knows enough to reject the wrong and choose the right**" (Isaiah 7:16 NIV84).

Both passages cited above hint at the idea of an age of accountability, but I want to emphasize that there is nothing in the Bible that specifically outlines when that accountability begins. Furthermore, there are no passages that specifically promise that a child who dies will be instantly granted entrance into heaven. Some would disagree, citing the statement by Jesus in which He said, "Let the little children come to me and do not hinder them, for to such belongs the kingdom of heaven" (Matthew 19:14). However, this is one of many passages where Jesus uses an analogy of a childlike heart to highlight what it takes to enter heaven (see Matthew 18:2–3). He is not saying that heaven is literally populated by children.

The comfort and confidence of knowing that a child is in heaven with God is not going to be fully satisfied by some

246   PASTOR, I HAVE A QUESTION

proof text from Scripture. Instead, this kind of confidence comes from knowing the character of God. To know God personally and intimately is to know with assurance that He can be trusted. In such cases, I personally rely on these truths about God:

1. God is love (1 John 4:8). I know this statement may sound trite, but its implications remain our biggest reason for having hope in the midst of those things in life which seem horribly unfair and leave us with nothing but questions. When death visits a small child, we can have the absolute confidence of knowing that God cares even more than we do about the passing of that child. Furthermore, He is unhindered in His ability to express His love toward them.

2. God can be trusted to do what is right. When Abraham was told that God was about to rain down judgment upon the cities of Sodom and Gomorrah (where his nephew Lot happened to be living), Abraham began to question God's mercy and forbearance. Finally, he posed this question to the Lord: "Will not the Judge of all the earth do right?" (Genesis 18:25 NIV). Abraham had confidence in the answer to that question, but sometimes I wonder if believers today possess that same confidence. God is the Judge of all the earth. Can we trust Him to make the absolute best decision in such matters? I believe we can, and that ought to fill us with hope.

I believe that upon death God accepts children into His presence without question. I believe so, not because I have a single passage of Scripture that I can point to, but because my confidence rests in the Person of God Himself — His faithfulness and mercy which I find nothing short of astounding.

ON DEATH AND GOING TO HEAVEN 247

Do people become angels after they die?

In a word, *no*. But you may have noticed at funerals that it's fairly common to hear a poem or a song that mentions the deceased person as having gone to heaven to become an angel. One obituary I once read for a child had a statement that said the little child had now become the family's personal guardian angel.

Where do these beliefs come from?

Hollywood has certainly perpetuated this idea in films, but in recent years it has even been popping up more and more in Christian circles. So, is there any biblical evidence that a person might become an angel?

None whatsoever!

Throughout the Scriptures, humans and angels are always distinctively different. We really don't know much about angels, such as when they were created — but we *do* know they are very different from human beings.

Below are some of the differences the Bible lists between humans and angels along with their corresponding Scripture references.

1. Humans have physical bodies. Angels do not.

Are not all angels ministering spirits sent to serve those who will inherit salvation? (Hebrews 1:14 NIV)

While humans are corporeal (possessing a body of flesh and bone), the Bible tells us here that angels are "spirits." There are certainly examples in Scripture where angels have taken on human form, but they remain spirit-beings.

248 PASTOR, I HAVE A QUESTION

The passage in Hebrews also tells us that angels are servants sent to minister to "those who will inherit salvation" meaning, humans. This further distinguishes angels from humans.

2. Humans can die. Angels cannot.

...and they can no longer die; for they are like the angels. They are God's children, since they are children of the resurrection. (Luke 20:36 NIV)

In the passage above, Jesus refers to believers who are made alive in the resurrection as being "like the angels" since they can no longer be touched by death. Jesus doesn't say we will become angels — only that with respect to death, we will be *like* the angels.

Since angels are spirit-beings with no physical bodies, they cannot experience a physical death. They are eternal. Human beings are also created to be eternal but our physical bodies grow old, wear out and die. That part of us which is spirit remains alive.

3. Humans can be saved (forgiven of their sins and promised eternal life). Angels cannot.

For surely it is not angels he helps, but Abraham's descendants. (Hebrews 2:16 NIV)

When the God of the universe came to live on the earth, He was born as a human baby in the person of Jesus of Nazareth. He became a human because He came to represent humans, not angels. When He died on the cross He did not die for the sins of angels, but for the sins of human beings.

4. Humans can become heirs of God and joint heirs with Christ. These same blessings are not available to angels.

It is not to angels that he has subjected the world to come, about which we are speaking. (Hebrews 2:5 NIV)

One of the most wonderful blessings that we find in Scripture centers around the promises of God that are directed toward all who place their faith in Jesus Christ for the forgiveness of sins. These promises are far too many to list here but suffice it to say none of them are directed to angels.

God's angels are wonderful beings and they have important work to do in the plan of the Lord. But it is vital that we never confuse the function and ministry of angels with that of human beings.

It can be said with clear and unquestioning sincerity that God has a much better and bigger plan for humans than merely becoming angels. He has invited us to become His beloved children — which He makes possible through His Son, Jesus Christ.

Do we enter a state of "soul sleep" after death?

In the Bible there are many usages of the word *sleep* when referring to physical death. Here are some examples:

Then David slept with his fathers and was buried in the city of David. (1 Kings 2:10)

To the church in Thessalonica the Apostle Paul wrote:

But we do not want you to be uninformed, brothers, about those who are asleep, that you may not grieve as others do who have no hope. For since we believe that Jesus died and rose again, even so, through Jesus, God will bring with him those who have fallen asleep. For this we declare to you by a word from the Lord, that we who are alive, who are left until the coming of the Lord, will not precede those who have fallen asleep. (1 Thessalonians 4:13–15)

You can see here why many people accept the idea of "soul sleep." Three times in three verses Paul uses the term "asleep" to describe those who have died in Christ. But we have to take note that "sleep," "asleep," and other sleep-related terms function as euphemisms for *death* — where the physical body takes on the appearance of sleep.

We need to have a good biblical reason to consider that euphemism is being used in all these cases, otherwise we're just projecting our personal opinion. There are very good reasons to reject the idea of soul sleep. The first comes from the Apostle Paul who, when speaking of life both in the body and out of the body, wrote:

Therefore we are always confident and know that as long as we are at home in the body we are away from the Lord. For we live by faith, not by sight. We are confident, I say, and would prefer to be away from the body and at home with the Lord. (2 Corinthians 5:6–8 NIV)

Paul declared that he much preferred to be absent from the body because that meant he would be present with the Lord.

But perhaps the best reason to not embrace the idea of soul sleep is a story that Jesus told about the death of two men (see Luke 16). It concerns a wealthy man and a diseased beggar by the name of Lazarus. In this story, both men suffer physical death. Lazarus is transported by the angels of God to a place of comfort and the wealthy man is sent immediately to a place of suffering where he awaits judgment.

In the case of both of these men, they are fully conscious and aware of their present circumstances and surroundings. Since there's no reason to consider this story anything other than a telling of real events, it shows that Jesus taught something other than soul sleep. And since His is an unimpugnable authority, I believe we are left with some very concrete reasons to believe that the human soul does not sleep after death.

252 PASTOR, I HAVE A QUESTION

Do stillborn babies go to heaven?

Over the years I've had the occasion to officiate at funerals and graveside services for infants who were either stillborn or lived only a few minutes or hours after birth. The question that is naturally on everyone's mind is whether we will be reunited with the children we've lost.

If you're looking for a single Bible passage that says "all little babies go to heaven" — you're going to be disappointed because such a passage doesn't exist. But that doesn't mean the Bible doesn't give us valuable insight that will help us to reach an informed conclusion.

So, what *does* the Bible say?

In 2 Samuel 12, we're told of a time when a baby born to David's wife Bathsheba died. While the child was sick, David fasted and prayed. But after the baby died, David said:

"While the child was still alive, I fasted and wept, for I said, 'Who knows whether the LORD will be gracious to me, that the child may live?' But now he is dead. Why should I fast? Can I bring him back again? I shall go to him, but he will not return to me." (vv. 22–23)

In the midst of his grief, David expressed a confidence that one day he would be reunited with his child, obviously refer-ring to a time after his own physical death. Where did David get this information? Was it just a belief of his time? I think not. David was a man with unique insights into God and His plan for mankind. Much later, Peter declared that David "was a prophet" (Acts 2:30). I believe David was speaking with prophetic insight when he declared by faith that he would see his child again.

The other thing we must keep at the forefront when considering such questions is the character of God. By knowing God's character, we can fill in the blanks on many issues in life that are not directly addressed in the Bible. One passage I love to remember is Micah 7:18 which says that God "delight(s) to show mercy" (NIV) or as the ESV renders it, the Lord "delights in steadfast love."

So, you have a little baby who, for whatever reason, was either stillborn or didn't live long past birth. And you also have a God who literally *delights* to show mercy and steadfast love and is perfectly fair and just. What do you end up with?

Hope!

Our God is good! And we can *always* trust Him to do the right thing.

Can we talk to our departed loved ones?

It's hard to lose someone close to you because it leaves a huge empty space in your heart. The closer you were to the person, the more intensely you feel the loss. Therefore, it's quite natural to want that special connection to live on even when that loved one has died.

There are people called "mediums" who claim to be able to help you reestablish communication with those who are departed. Mediums were present in biblical times just like today, but God strictly forbade His people from going to them and using their services. There are several passages that speak of this (see Leviticus 19:31; 20:27; Deuteronomy 18:10–11; Isaiah 8:19).

254   PASTOR, I HAVE A QUESTION

There is nothing in the Bible that suggests that those who have died are in any way able to hear or communicate with those still alive on earth. There are certainly people who believe they can communicate with the dead, but their belief is not based on any biblical revelation.

Sometimes people will point to a story recorded in 1 Samuel 28 as a proof that speaking to the dead is acceptable. Even though God had forbidden the Israelites from consulting a medium, King Saul foolishly attempted to do so to call up the spirit of the prophet Samuel and ask him for counsel concerning his desperate situation. The Lord graciously allowed Samuel, even though he was dead, to deliver one final prophecy to Saul — a prophecy of his own impending death. This story does not teach that the Bible is okay with speaking to and consulting the dead as some naively believe. (The verses I listed earlier will further clarify this point.)

God understands all about the emptiness in your heart created by the loss of your departed loved one. I would encourage you to talk to Him about it.

How will we recognize one another in heaven before we receive our new bodies?

The reason you're asking this question is because here on earth we are so accustomed to identifying people and objects using our five senses. When I see someone I recognize, I conclude that I know that person. We assume it will be the same when we're with the Lord. But you need to understand that when we shed our physical bodies, we will not have less than we do now. We will have *much* more — more insight, more understanding, and more abilities. Our ability to recognize people will go *far beyond* anything we know now and will *not* be determined merely by sight.

Have you ever read the passage in Matthew 17 where Jesus took Peter, James, and John up onto the mountain where Moses and Elijah appeared and had a conversation with Jesus? If you read the passage again, you'll see that Peter began speaking about the presence of Elijah and Moses prior to anyone actually telling him *who* those two men were. How did he know it was Elijah and how did he know it was Moses? There were no photographs back then and yet he instantly knew who they were and called them by name.

The reason he knew them is that in the presence of the Lord there is knowledge — a knowledge that transcends anything we have today through intellectual learning or observation through our five physical senses (Isaiah 11:9).

So, don't worry. When you see your mom again, you'll *know* it's her!

Chapter 18

QUESTIONS ABOUT THE BIBLE

- Did someone write the Bible or did it just appear? 257

- Is one method of Bible translation better than the other? 258

- Which Bible translation should I be reading? 263

Did someone write the Bible or did it just appear?

The Bible was written by some 40 different authors over a period of about 1,500+ years. Many of the books of the Bible reveal their authorship but others do not. This is true for the Old and the New Testaments. The authors we know of include kings, prophets, church leaders, and even a doctor.

The Bible didn't just magically appear. It was written by individuals. Some of them just set out to record historical events while others took up the pen because they were conscious of the Holy Spirit moving them to write down what they believed was a message from heaven.

The Old Testament writings are those which were (and still are) accepted by both Jews and Christians as authoritative and divinely inspired by God. Our best claim to the authority of the Old Testament is that Jesus Himself often quoted from these writings and clearly accepted them as having a divine origin.

The New Testament books are largely the writings of the original Apostles or those who lived and served with them. These letters circulated among the early churches and were accepted early on to be of equal weight with the Old Testament.

Is one method of Bible translation better than the other?

I want to make it clear right off that I'm not a Bible scholar. I'm a Bible teacher with a passion to make the Word of God understandable and along those lines I have some thoughts on Bible translations.

Let me also add quickly that we are blessed beyond blessed today with so many Bible translations available at our fingertips. When I was a student in Bible college and I wanted to read a different Bible translation, it meant a trip to my local Christian bookstore to buy it. Later, when technology made digital copies of God's Word available, we still had to purchase the version of our choice. Today, with apps like You-Version, we can now read pretty much any Bible translation we want — and they're all FREE. It's really incredible!

But that still raises the question: which one is best for you? To answer that, it might help to know how Bibles are translated.

Methods of Bible Translation
Have you noticed that some Bible versions read very differently compared to others? Some sound pretty much like the way you and I speak in everyday conversation and others are a bit more formal and rigid. The reason for that difference is the method of translation that each translating committee decides to take when setting out to translate God's Word. There are essentially two different methods.

The first is called the "**formal equivalence**" or "**word-for-word**" approach. In this method, every effort is made to keep both the word order and sentence structure of the original Hebrew or Greek. Bibles that use this method include the ESV, NKJV, and NASB. These are the Bibles that

QUESTIONS ABOUT THE BIBLE   259

tend to sound a little rigid and often include words that you and I don't use in common day-to-day conversation.

Then we come to the second approach which is a "**functional equivalence**" or "**thought-for-thought**" rendering of the original text. This is also referred to as '**dynamic equivalence**' – in case you weren't confused enough already – and it's what you'll find in the International Children's Bible (ICB) and the New English Bible (NEB) just to name a couple. The goal of a thought-for-thought approach is to produce the most natural and readable style possible.

Then there are translations like the NIV, NLT, and NRSV which confuse the process even more by trying to balance the concepts of word-for-word and thought-for-thought in a single translation. (Note: Bibles like *The Message* and *The Living Bible* are not translations but paraphrases.)

For decades I read and taught from the NIV (1984 revision). I really loved that Bible, and still do. It remains both readable and accurate. My first NIV came out of the lost and found at the church I was attending back in the early 1980s. It was a paperback and I used it and wrote in it until it was literally in tatters. Eventually I had to get a new Bible so I marched down to my local Christian bookstore and bought my very first NIV Thompson Chain-Reference Bible. It was very cool!

The Problem with Word-for-word
Have you ever noticed that Bible translations that claim to be word-for-word choose different English words to translate the same text? How can that be? I mean, if they're rendering a passage word-for-word, then their translations should be identical, right?

Wrong. And the reason is that many times Hebrew and Greek words may require multiple English words to accurately

260 PASTOR, I HAVE A QUESTION

convey their meaning. Each translating committee then has to determine which English words they're going to use, and it does happen that the words used by one translating committee are very different from the words used by another committee.

Here's an example of how the meaning of a word can vary:

Jesus answered and said to him, "Truly, truly, I say to you, unless one is born again he cannot see the kingdom of God." John 3:3 (NASB95)

Seems straightforward. But although the Greek word that is translated here as "born" occurs some 41 times in the NASB, it is also rendered as:

- father,

- begotten,

- became the father of,

...and approximately 10 other English words or phrases! Crazy, huh?

Greek and Hebrew words can have variations in definition depending on the context of the passage. It's up to the translators to determine that context and then choose the English word (or words) they feel best expresses the original meaning. Obviously, different translating committees choose different words, and this takes the whole idea of word-for-word and tosses it up into the air.

Here's the point: word-for-word translations are wonderful and incredibly useful for studying the Scriptures, but they're not always the most effective way to convey the meaning of the passage.

QUESTIONS ABOUT THE BIBLE 261

Check out this example to see how 1 Kings 2:10 is rendered in these different translations:

- **KJV:** So David slept with his fathers, and was buried in the city of David.

- **NIV1984:** Then David rested with his fathers and was buried in the City of David.

- **NIV2011:** Then David rested with his ancestors and was buried in the City of David.

- **NLT:** Then David died and was buried with his ancestors in the City of David.

You can tell by reading all these different versions that the challenging phrase here is "**slept with his fathers**" which, by the way, is the most word-for-word accurate rendering of the original Hebrew. It was used in those days to refer to someone who died and was buried in the same area as his deceased relatives.

But does that word-for-word rendering really say it best? In our culture, the idea of sleeping with someone has a sexual connotation, but that's obviously not what the author was trying to say. For that reason, of the four translations listed, I find that the NLT probably does the best job of conveying the simple meaning by saying "David died." But it doesn't tell us everything, does it?

If I had my way as to how the translation would go, I would merge the NIV and NLT so that the verse reads this way: "**Then David died and was buried alongside his ancestors in Jerusalem, the City of David**." In this case, we have a sentence that contains everything the author wanted us to know, in a way that is clearly understood by a modern English-speaking reader.

262   PASTOR, I HAVE A QUESTION

Is there a danger to the thought-for-thought approach?

Even though I believe that a thought-for-thought translation often does a better job of conveying the meaning of the text, the method is not without its potential dangers. Questions arise, such as, how far should we go to make the passage easy to understand? And is it possible to go too far?

The answer is, unfortunately, yes.

Back in 2011, when the publishers of the New International Version (NIV) released their latest revision, I was troubled by some of the changes made to the text. Although I really like a thought-for-thought approach, the fact is, it doesn't always bring clarity to the passage and if you're not careful, it can do the opposite. Up until the 2011 revision, I had always felt that the NIV did a good job of giving the reader the meaning of the text without compromising accuracy. But with the latest changes, I think they stepped over the line by adopting a new gender-inclusive approach. That's why I switched to the ESV.

I'm not saying the new NIV is a bad translation. Not at all. I wouldn't hesitate to give a copy of the 2011 revision to someone who needed a Bible. But in terms of accuracy, I feel that the ESV, NASB, and NKJV do a better job of staying faithful to the text, despite their somewhat rigid and inflexible reading styles.

So what's the "best" translation?

I've always believed that the best translation is the one you read. With any of the modern English translations, it's hard to go wrong. And because they are all so easily available, you really don't have to choose. Even though you may have a favorite, I would encourage reading through the Bible every year in a different translation to get a well-rounded view of the Scriptures.

Glossary of Bible translation names:

ESV - English Standard Version

KJV – King James Version

NASB - New American Standard Bible

NIV - New International Version

NKJV - New King James Version

NLT - New Living Translation

NRSV – New Revised Standard Version

Which Bible translation should I be reading?

If a Bible is referred to as a "translation" that means a committee of scholars pored over the original language manuscripts in order to translate them into English. A paraphrase, on the other hand, does not involve a translating committee. The two most popular paraphrases of the Bible: *The Living Bible* and *The Message* are considered as "personal paraphrase" and in each case the work was done by one man rather than by a committee of scholars.

Take the English Standard Version for example. When the ESV was translated, the committee – which was made up of Greek and Hebrew scholars – painstakingly went over the original language texts, trying to determine the best English words to use. Same with the New International Version (NIV), the New King James Version (NKJV), and the New American Standard Bible (NASB). All these translations went back to the original languages.

Are there wording differences in modern English translations? Sure. Do those differences change the meaning of the text? Not at all. Regardless of which Bible translation you read you will always find that:

- God is always the Creator.

- God is always revealed as Father, Son, and Holy Spirit.

- Jesus is always God's Son, born of a virgin.

- Jesus is always the Son of God.

- The cross of Christ is always revealed to be the only way we can be saved; and

- Jesus is always coming back.

I will repeat, there are *never* any variations to the doctrines and teachings of the Bible regardless of which version you read. So, which version of the Bible should you be reading? You should read the version that works best for you. With the excellent major English translations available today, you really can't go wrong.

Chapter 19

MISCELLANEOUS QUESTIONS

- How old is the earth? 267

- Is it okay to be re-baptized? 267

- Can you explain what Lent is all about? 268

- Why do we say we believe in the Catholic Church in the Apostle's Creed? 268

- Are Catholics considered Christians? 269

- Will Mormons and Catholics go to heaven? 271

- Is the Seventh Day Adventist Church a cult? 273

- Why does Satan oppose God when he knows he will ultimately fail? 273

- How can we recognize spiritual attacks? 274

- Are angels still among us? 274

266   PASTOR, I HAVE A QUESTION

- Is it wrong to use bread made with yeast in Communion? 275

- Am I allowed to partake in Communion even though I do not attend a church? 276

- Why is the Apostle John known as "the beloved"? 277

- How is it possible that Satanic forces could hinder the Lord from getting His message to Daniel? 278

How old is the earth?

According to Google, **4.54 billion years**.

The theory of a very old earth is considered as fact by a fairly large population, especially among those in the scientific community. But there are also many reputable individuals who are skeptical about how proponents of an "old earth" have arrived at those dates. The only biblical method to deduce the age of the earth would be to read various biblical accounts and attempt to compile a chronology based on life spans and so forth. Many have endeavored to do this and the result has been a figure somewhere around 6,000 years. (Quite a difference from 4.5 billion, eh?)

The website *Answers in Genesis* has compiled some excellent information on this topic and I encourage you to check it out.

Is it okay to be re-baptized?

The Bible does not specifically give us an answer. Over the years I have talked to dozens of believers who either consented to water baptism at an age when their understanding and appreciation of water baptism was incomplete, or were baptized into a church which they later came to realize was unbiblical. In such cases I see nothing wrong with being baptized once again.

Can you explain what Lent is all about?

Lent is a 40-day tradition that was started by Christians many years ago with the goal of helping believers prepare for the celebration of the resurrection of Jesus. It begins on Ash Wednesday and ends the Saturday before Easter.

Lent is typically observed by churches that are more liturgical in practice (churches that follow ritual and tradition), and involves a 40-day period of fasting, repentance, and reflection leading up to the celebration of Easter. Modern Evangelical churches typically do not observe Lent since they tend to de-emphasize extra-biblical traditions.

Why do we say we believe in the Catholic Church in the Apostle's Creed?

Many people hear the Apostle's Creed and wonder why we're declaring our belief in Catholicism. But the statement in the Apostle's Creed which says, "I believe in...the holy catholic church" has nothing whatsoever to do with Roman Catholicism. The word catholic originated from a Greek word that means "universal." The creed therefore is saying, "I believe in the universal Body of Christ." Roman Catholicism, therefore, is not at all being mentioned in that creed.

Are Catholics considered Christians?

Roman Catholicism is fundamentally considered part of the overall expression of Christianity but there are significant differences between Roman Catholicism and historic biblical Christianity.

For starters, Roman Catholicism is centered around a single spiritual leader — the Pope. Biblical Christianity has no central figure because the Bible discourages it. When the Apostle Paul wrote to the Corinthian believers, he discouraged them from elevating one church leader over another, saying:

For when one says, "I follow Paul," and another, "I follow Apollos," are you not being merely human? What then is Apollos? What is Paul? Servants through whom you believed, as the Lord assigned to each. I planted, Apollos watered, but God gave the growth. So neither he who plants nor he who waters is anything, but only God who gives the growth. (1 Corinthians 3:4–7)

Because the Pope possesses the same authority as the inspired Scriptures, many "dogmas" have emerged from Roman Catholicism that are nowhere found in the Bible. These include:

- Purgatory as a place of "working off" sins after death

- Designating some sins as "venial" and others as "mortal"

- References to Mary as the "mother of God"

- The sinless condition of Mary

- The worship of Mary and prayers directed to her

- The qualifications of sainthood

270   PASTOR, I HAVE A QUESTION

- Prayers to the saints

- The requirement of confessing one's sins to a priest

- The requirement of celibacy for priests and nuns

- Using the title "Father" when addressing priests

- The elevation of tradition alongside the authority of Scripture

The list goes on. Again, I want to make it clear that *none* of these beliefs finds corroborative standing in any of the 66 books which make up the Protestant Bible and several of them stand in direct contradiction to those Scriptures.

Frankly, the only difference that *really* matters surrounds the question of how a person is saved. Unfortunately, Roman Catholicism has added layers on top of the original message of receiving and accepting the finished work of Jesus on the cross. That alone sets it apart from biblical Christianity and looms as the largest and most dangerous of all the differences between the two.

According to Roman Catholicism, "justifying grace" is activated upon Catholic baptism and through the sacraments. However, this grace can be gradually lost through venial sins or forfeited completely by mortal sins.

The Apostle Paul made it clear in his letter to the Galatians that when you add "works" on top of the Gospel (which is exactly what Roman Catholicism has done), you end up with "no Gospel at all" (Galatians 1:6–7 NIV).

I do not subscribe to the belief that Catholics cannot possibly be Christians any more than I would say that all Baptists are Christians. Both statements are inaccurate generalizations since the biblical definition of a Christian is someone who is trusting in the finished work of Jesus' sacrificial death on the cross. If I meet someone who confesses Christ as the only way to be saved, I know I am talking to a Christian, regardless of that person's affiliation.

Will Mormons and Catholics go to heaven?

The Bible's teaching is clear. The only means of getting to heaven (having eternal life) is to believe that Jesus Christ died on the cross bearing the penalty of our sin, and to accept His sacrifice on our behalf. This is all predicated on these simple truths:

1. Man is born into sin and is spiritually cut off from God (Ephesians 2:1).

2. As a sinner, man is under God's direct wrath (Ephesians 2:3) and the consequences of man's sin is death (Romans 6:23).

3. It is not possible to earn a place in heaven by living a good life or by observing any sacraments or pursuing religious goals (Romans 3:20). Forgiveness of sins is referred to in the Bible as a "gift," meaning it is given apart from anything a person can do to earn it (Ephesians 2:8–9).

4. Jesus Christ is the Creator God (Colossians 1:16) who came to earth as a man so that He might take the punishment that we deserved from God (1 Timothy 1:15).

272 PASTOR, I HAVE A QUESTION

> 5. Eternal life is granted to all who receive the sacrifice of Jesus on their behalf and place their faith in His ability to save them from their sin (John 1:12). To those who truly believe, God sends His Holy Spirit by which we are born again (1 Peter 1:3; John 1:13).

This is what the Bible calls the Gospel or *good news*. And it is most certainly that, because it reveals to us that forgiveness of sins comes as a result of God's promise — *not* as the result of being good or observing religious rites or services.

So, do the teachings of Mormonism and Roman Catholicism create barriers for people to understand this good news? Yes, I believe they do.

Mormonism teaches another Gospel altogether, and Roman Catholicism has heaped hundreds and hundreds of years of tradition and dogma on top of the Gospel so that it no longer resembles what the Apostle Paul preached. But to confidently say that a Mormon or a Catholic will *not* enter heaven depends on how deeply they have been indoctrinated by those groups. (There are many who call themselves LDS or even Catholic who quite honestly have little or no idea what those belief systems teach.) So, is it possible for someone who considers themselves LDS or Roman Catholic to discover the Gospel and so be saved? Absolutely!

God doesn't save people according to what church they attend. His only standard is whether or not we are trusting His Son completely for forgiveness. That, and that alone, is all that matters.

Is the Seventh Day Adventist Church a cult?

In most cases I would say no. It all depends on how heavily SDA adherents rely on the writings of Ellen G. White, a co-founder of the movement. When White's writings are viewed as inspired alongside Scripture, you could say that Seventh Day Adventism certainly has elements that are consistent with a cult. However, there are SDA members who do their best to stick only to the Bible. This means they do not follow White's writings or in extreme cases, consider her writings as uninspired commentary. The only thing that really sets them apart from other Christians is that they worship on Saturdays.

In my opinion, it is impossible and even reckless to refer to Seventh Day Adventism as a cult since the characteristics of a cult are not visible in all expressions of that movement.

Why does Satan oppose God when he knows he will ultimately fail?

We don't know with absolute certainty what Satan knows and what he doesn't know. Either way, Satan's efforts and actions always spring from his nature. He doesn't just *do* evil, he *is* evil. That means he can't do or be otherwise. Darkness will always hate and try to eradicate the light simply because darkness is evil. It needs no more reason than that. Jesus said of the devil:

He was a murderer from the beginning, and does not stand in the truth, because there is no truth in him. When he lies, he speaks out of his own character, for he is a liar and the father of lies. (John 8:44)

Jesus said that Satan "speaks out of his own character." That means he lies because he *is* a liar. He murders because he *is* a murderer. He seeks to do evil because he *is* evil. Satan is what he is, and all his actions stem from that awful reality.

How can we recognize spiritual attacks?

It is impossible for us to distinguish between a spiritual attack and merely a difficult circumstance resulting from living in a fallen world. These can only be discerned with the help of the Holy Spirit.

True spiritual attacks can come in *any* form, but we're never told to focus on spiritual attacks. We're told to focus on **being ready** for anything the enemy might throw at us by putting on the full armor of God. Our focus should be on the power of God rather than the attacks of the enemy.

Are angels still among us?

Since we are told that angels are "ministering spirits sent to serve those who will inherit salvation" (Hebrews 1:14 NIV), there is every reason to believe that angels are all around us and are active in our lives. I would recommend the book

Angels: God's Secret Agents by Billy Graham. It is a wonderful book packed with real-life testimonies of the intervention of angels in people's lives.

On whether angels still bring messages from God — that is certainly possible; but with the unprecedented access we have these days to God's Word in printed and digital form, there's very little reason for angels to bring a message from God. His message is all around us if we would just pick up a Bible and start reading.

Is it wrong to use bread made with yeast in Communion?

It's true that God forbade the Israelites to use or even possess yeast (or leaven) in their homes during the eight days of Passover and Feast of Unleavened Bread. It's also true that yeast was a biblical symbol for sin. It became a valuable word picture for the Jews in understanding the way sin can spread throughout our lives.

But it is *not* true that Communion bread must be unleavened in order to be acceptable. I say this based on two important points:

First, it is <u>incorrect</u> to assume that the ceremonial requirements for Israel's worship observances transfer to the New Testament Church.

Many Christians assume that the Old Covenant regulations and prohibitions carry over to New Testament believers. As you can imagine, this has resulted in huge and long-lasting debates: Should we still worship on the seventh-day Sabbath? What about requirements for clothing or food laws?

It is important to remember that, as the Body of Christ, we are *not* under the Mosaic Covenant and the ceremonial regulations given to Israel are *not* in force for the Church.

Second, there is nothing in the New Testament that suggests Communion bread must be unleavened.

Yes, Jesus and His disciples ate unleavened bread during the Last Supper, but that's because they were observing Passover. We must remember that Communion is *not* a recreation of Passover — it is a remembrance of Christ's death on the cross. Therefore, the requirements and prohibitions placed on Israel for observing Passover *do not* transfer to our observance of Communion.

Am I allowed to partake in Communion even though I do not attend a church?

More and more Christians are "churching" online, meaning, they are receiving ministry of the Word from various internet sources. Even our church is streaming our services live and archiving our teachings both on our own website and YouTube. There appears to be a real hunger for God's Word, as evidenced by the steadily increasing number of people tuning in to our every upload.

So, what happens when the live service you're watching includes a time of Communion? Is there any way for someone tuning in online to participate? Sure! Why not? Grab some bread (or whatever you have on hand) and something to drink, and by all means join in. The point of Communion is to remember the death of Jesus on our behalf. If you're watching from home, I don't see any reason why you shouldn't feel free to partake. Whatever objections someone might have about online participation in a Communion service will most likely be rooted in church tradition rather than the Word of God. So unless anyone can show a biblical reason why you should not participate, I say go for it.

Why is the Apostle John known as "the beloved"?

It's true that John referred to himself as "**the disciple whom Jesus loved**" on several occasions. A typical follow-up to that question is whether we can conclude that Jesus loved him more than the other disciples.

Here are some important facts to consider:

First, John was the only one who used this title for himself. Technically speaking, he wasn't publicly "known as the beloved." The title "the disciple whom Jesus loved" therefore, can be regarded as a nickname he applied to himself. Second, John never explained why he used that title, nor did he explain what it meant.

I think we can be certain that John never intended to convey that Jesus loved him more than anyone else. After all, this is the same man who wrote down the words, "**For God so loved the world that he gave his only begotten Son.**" John understood the love of God and I don't believe he saw himself as a unique or special recipient of the love of Jesus.

The other thing we need to understand is that there were many sayings and statements used in antiquity that translate very poorly into modern English. I believe this is one of them. I think John was using this statement in place of his own name as a way of simply referring to himself as one who was loved by Jesus. Not the *only* one, mind you, or even the one *best* loved, but simply "one loved by the Lord."

I think it's a name that any of us can take on after coming to the realization that we are the unlikely recipients of God's unconditional and life-transforming love. John was so taken with the idea that Jesus gave Himself as a sacrifice, that he spoke of that love in a personal and tender way: "I am one who is loved by Jesus." Whatever exclusivity we hear in that statement is, I believe, more of an irregularity in the translation from ancient to Greek to modern English.

How is it possible that Satanic forces could hinder the Lord from getting His message to Daniel?

Believers know that God is all-powerful, so this passage really presents a problem. But come to think of it, there is so much we don't know concerning how things work in the spiritual realm and how mankind's sin has affected the world, both spiritual and physical.

Your question echoes a line of thought that, in essence,

MISCELLANEOUS QUESTIONS 279

takes an attribute of God or cites His will and then asks why things or circumstances don't necessarily reflect what *we know* to be true of the Lord. This manner of thinking is also often the backbone of questions about many other things such as salvation. One might ask, "If God desires all mankind to be saved (2 Peter 3:9) then why isn't everyone saved?" Obviously, God has chosen to honor the freewill that He created mankind to have; and yet on the surface, it seems as if man's freewill actually trumps the will of God. (This has caused people much consternation.)

It is the same principle in the Daniel passage: *How could a demonic principality slow down the Lord God even for a second, let alone 21 days?* Well, again, there are things that God has chosen to honor for a season and if men choose to worship demonic forces, He will allow those forces to reign and exercise their authority for as long as He determines. But make no mistake — their reign is limited, and there will come a day when all such principalities and powers will be overthrown completely.

Printed in Great Britain
by Amazon

20 Air Fryer recipes for beginners

Laura Venables

Copyright © 2024 Laura Venables
All rights reserved.
ISBN: 9798876369642